The GOSPEL
of SECOND
CHANCES

The GOSPEL of SECOND CHANCES

LLOYD D. NEWELL

DESERET
BOOK

Salt Lake City, Utah

Visit us at DeseretBook.com

Library of Congress Cataloging-in-Publication Data

Newell, Lloyd D., author.
  The Gospel of second chances / Lloyd D. Newell.
      pages   cm
  Includes bibliographical references and index.
    ISBN 978-1-60641-713-3 (hardbound : alk. paper)
 1. Repentance—The Church of Jesus Christ of Latter-day Saints.   2. Christian life—Mormon authors.   3. The Church of Jesus Christ of Latter-day Saints—Doctrines.
    I. Title.
    BX8656.N486 2012
    234'.5—dc23   2012041708

Printed in the United States of America
Publishers Printing, Salt Lake City, UT

10   9   8   7   6   5   4   3   2   1

CONTENTS

CONTENTS

PREFACE

This book is about hope in Jesus Christ, about why we have every reason to believe that we can change and start anew. I believe it is a message we all need, no matter who we are, what we have or have not done, or what stage of life we may be in.

The love of God is the most powerful force in the universe and the most joyous thing we can experience on this earth. But we sometimes forget *who* we are and *whose* we are while traveling the road of mortality. This love of God and hope in Christ whisper to our hearts the sweet truth that we can be forgiven, we can begin again, and we can press forward by holding steadfastly to Christ. His mercy is the source and substance of our faith and hope.

My sincere prayer is that this volume will assist us in remembering and reinforcing the hope and truth and power found in the gospel of second chances.

ACKNOWLEDGMENTS

An author can never fully acknowledge all the people and stories and events that helped bring to print a book or influence the author's life. Nonetheless, I express profound appreciation for the myriad people—past and present—who have positively shaped both my writing and my life.

As always, Deseret Book has been helpful and supportive all along the way. In particular, Jana Erickson, Suzanne Brady, Heather Ward, and Rachael Ward have offered wise counsel, valuable encouragement, and their much-needed editorial eyes and professional expertise.

I am particularly indebted to two invaluable people: my friend and editor extraordinaire, Ted Barnes, who shaped the manuscript and provided exceptional editorial assistance; and to my beloved wife, Karmel, who always helps my writing and my life become better and who is a constant example of Christian goodness.

In addition, I gratefully acknowledge the countless people from all walks of life whose stories of second chances continue to unfold and inspire. Several of those stories are told in this short work, some with names of individuals, circumstances, and other details changed to maintain privacy. Innumerable other stories remain yet untold but deeply appreciated.

CHAPTER 1

A MESSAGE OF HOPE

As Christ was raised up from the dead by the glory of the Father,
even so we also should walk in newness of life.

ROMANS 6:4

During the last few weeks of a cold, snowy winter, hungry deer attacked the ivy in front of our home, leaving nothing but what looked like tangled brown sticks. My wife nearly cried when she surveyed the damage. We feared that the tender plants were beyond repair. We thought we would have to pull the ivy out, start over, and replant. We decided to save that somber task until the weather changed and tried to forget about the assault to our landscape for the time being.

When spring's warmth finally arrived and we revisited the ivy, we could hardly believe our eyes: broken vines had somehow mended, and tiny buds appeared. In time, those little buds flourished into beautiful, verdant leaves. Today, several springs later, the ivy is robust and continues to spread its leafy sprouts across our home.

Though it seemed miraculous to us, the regeneration of our ivy plant was actually not that unusual. Similar miracles happen every year all over the world as spring follows winter in an unceasing and marvelous cycle of rebirth and rejuvenation. It's an annual reminder that renewal can come, positive change can happen, and hope is at the center of everything. Grass that looks dead, brown, and beaten somehow thrives again. Bulbs buried in the dark soil send their shoots toward the light, and flowers triumph afresh. Hope is always part of the landscape. We joyously celebrate new life in nature, but we might also celebrate the new life that comes of another spiritual opportunity, a fresh start, a second chance.

A VOICE FOR HOPE

This book came as a result of seeing change and growth all around me for many years—in my yard and in myself. Like you, I've certainly needed to repent, and I most assuredly need forgiveness. I've experienced my share of heartache and difficulty. Like you, I've watched the miracle of second chances reveal itself time and time again. The essence of the gospel of Jesus Christ is that we can repent and be forgiven; we can endure disappointments and setbacks; we can and must go forward into the future with faith. Because I believe in the gospel of second chances, I believe in hope and faith, redemption and renewal, new birth and new life. Without trust in a loving Father and Son who make second chances possible, life would be most miserable.

We hear the expression "There are no guarantees in life." But here is one promise, one guarantee you can count on no matter where you are or what you have done: You can have a second chance. Just as a disobedient child says to his mother, "I promise I'll do better next time" and "Can I try again?" as we get older we may wonder and ask, "Is there hope for me?" and "Can I really start over?" We've probably all felt that way from time to time. We've fallen short and longed for another chance, a fresh start, a new beginning. We've all wished we could take back something we've said or done, rewind time, and try again. Justice and fairness will always have their claim, but so will mercy and second chances.

I suspect that most everyone who reads this book genuinely wants to live a good life. We strive to do our best; we endeavor to live the gospel. But we all need second chances. Sometimes we question if a relationship can ever be mended or a broken heart healed. Sometimes we are painfully aware of our shortcomings and weaknesses and wonder if we will ever be good enough or ever measure up to all the Lord expects of us. Such doubts are natural and common, but they are not beneficial. As the English poet Tennyson urged, "Cleave ever to the sunnier side of doubt."[1]

We live in a cynical time, when optimism is confused with naiveté and surliness is mistaken for sophistication. Part of my purpose in writing this book is to advocate for hope. In particular, I want to persuade you to believe in and hope for second chances—for yourself and for those you love.

So many people wonder: How do we overcome our fallen nature and really change for the better? Can we stay faithful and strong in this sinful and difficult world? Is hope truly possible? If I've made a mistake—perhaps many mistakes—can God still use me, or will I be consigned to the dustbin of life? Is it too late for me? Can I really begin again? Are second chances, comebacks, and do-overs really possible?

Hope is the flame that brightens even the longest of nights. A story about a Jewish prisoner in a Nazi concentration camp illustrates how important it is to keep hope alive. On the first night of Hanukkah (which, in most parts of the world, falls at the darkest time of the year), Jews traditionally light the first candle in their menorah. Not having any provisions for such a celebration, the prisoner saved a scrap of bread from his meager meal and dipped it in grease from his dinner dish. Later, after saying the appropriate prayer, he lit his makeshift candle.

His son did not understand. He asked, "Father, that was food you burned. We have so little of it. Wouldn't we have been better off eating it?"

The father replied, "My son, people can live for a week without food, but they cannot live for one day without hope."[2]

Hope leads us to see ourselves—and others—as children of a loving Heavenly Father. It helps us trust the Lord, who, as the Psalmist said, is a light who can dispel fear (see Psalm 27:1). When the night seems particularly dark, we can light a candle in our hearts; we can pray to a loving Father in Heaven who has given us the promise of hope.

When we choose to hope despite our doubts, when we decide to trust in spite of our fears, we begin to feel power in the present and faith in the future. The sunnier side of doubt leads us to see the world through a lens of expectation and confidence.

But truthfully, hope is so much more than positive thinking

or an optimistic outlook. True hope is found deep in the heart and is expressed through meaningful work and worthwhile activity. It is manifested in service, sacrifice, and selflessness. It is when hope becomes an active, "lively hope" that we truly discover a higher power and greater purpose in life (1 Peter 1:3). Then our hope becomes an assurance that things can change for the better—that *we* can change for the better.

Some time ago, our ward bade farewell to a young man who departed to serve a mission. We had not seen much of him from the age of about sixteen to eighteen as he struggled with various problems. His family was heartbroken during that time, and his ward family was concerned. But in time, and through serious repentance, he got to the point where he was worthy and prepared and excited to serve the Lord in the mission field. His farewell was very emotional for him, his family, and the ward. We all had been pulling and praying for him.

In his remarks, he humbly asked forgiveness of any whom he had offended. He sincerely thanked his family and the ward for giving him a second chance. Over and over again he said in his testimony, "It's never too late to change. . . . There's always hope." He expressed his gratitude and love for the Lord and His mercy, for the Atonement, and for the miracle of forgiveness. He exhorted others, especially the youth, not to do as he had done but to hold onto the iron rod and stay strong in the gospel. He would never be able to reclaim those lost years, so there was remorse mixed with the joy that overflowed from his heart. Hope was his central message. I don't think there was a dry eye in the congregation as we all witnessed the power of the gospel of second chances. We felt the truth of President Thomas S. Monson's encouraging words: "Be of good cheer. The future is as bright as your faith."[3]

Sometimes, in the middle of a dark and cold winter, it is difficult to believe that spring's light and renewal will ever return. Likewise, when we're in the midst of heartache, when our weaknesses seem to outweigh our strengths and our difficulties overshadow our joys, it's easy to lose hope for today and wonder about tomorrow. While spring's warmth seems distant during the winters of our lives, we can hope and trust that it will surely come, things will work out, positive change is forthcoming, and life will go on—everlastingly. I love the hopeful assurance of the hymn "When Faith Endures":

> *I will not doubt, I will not fear;*
> *God's love and strength are always near.*
> *His promised gift helps me to find*
> *An inner strength and peace of mind.*[4]

My heartfelt message is that no matter the circumstances, we can find that "inner strength and peace of mind." Second chances, comebacks, and do-overs are both possible and wonderful. Fortunately for us mistake- and sin-prone humans, the Lord allows U-turns and turning points and opportunities to make things right.

YOU Are the Audience for This Book

Before I get too far into this subject, I should make a clarification about second chances. The tone of this book, so far, may have led you to the conclusion that the second chances of which I speak are principally for those in the "darkest abyss" of tragic sin (Mosiah 27:29). Perhaps you are thinking to yourself, "It's so nice that Brother Newell is writing this book for people who need a second chance in life. Heaven knows there are a lot of people like that. I can even think of a loved one who needs this message. Thank goodness I've been blessed to avoid such dreadful tragedy in my life."

In fact, while writing this book, I spoke to a good friend about second chances. She is a stalwart Latter-day Saint with a strong testimony of the gospel. She said, much to my surprise, "I don't need a second chance."

She wasn't being self-righteous or prideful. In her mind, she supposed that this book is intended for those who have wandered as prodigals in serious sin, those who have departed from the gospel path and now struggle to grasp once again the iron rod. She was clearly not part of that group and therefore concluded that the book would not have any direct relevance for her.

Her comment made me think about second chances in a new way. It is my belief that we all need second (and third and fourth and . . .) chances, every one of us, for reasons large and small. This book is not just for prodigals, for those like Alma the Younger and Paul and Jonah of old—it's for each one of us.

A little later, we'll discuss the universality of the need for second chances in much more detail. For now, I invite you to consider yourself the primary audience for this book, and please forgive me if my descriptions of second chances sound more dramatic than the second chances you might need. My hope is that by the time you have finished reading this book not only will you recognize second chances in your own life but you will also see, as I have, that no description of this marvelous gift—however superlative it may seem—comes close to capturing its stunning majesty. It's simply something each of us has to experience—over and over again. This book is merely a sincere attempt to encourage the experience in as many of us as possible.

CHAPTER 2

THE GOSPEL'S
CENTRAL MESSAGE

The Atonement of Jesus Christ allows us to learn *from our experience*
without being condemned *by that experience.*

BRUCE C. HAFEN

I f you had only a few minutes to tell someone about the gospel
of Jesus Christ, what would you say? Of all the profound and
rich doctrines of the fulness of the gospel, which one would you
share?

A few years ago, I was sitting in Sunday School class when
the teacher began his lesson by asking a similar question: "What
is the most important message of the gospel?" Hands shot up,
and many answers were given: Christ died for us, we will be res-
urrected, the gospel has been restored, we have a living prophet,
priesthood power is again on the earth, we can talk with God
through prayer, scriptures are the revealed word of God. Other
worthy comments were made. I sat pondering which principle of
the gospel I would select as the most important.

When the comments slowed, and after a moment of silence,

a middle-aged brother who had experienced many of life's heart-aches, including an extended period of inactivity, said thoughtfully, "I believe that the most important message of the gospel is that we can change."

How true.

Although every principle of the gospel is important, and we each need different aspects emphasized at different times in our lives, what message could be more central and more universal than this: Through faith in Jesus Christ and by the enabling power of the infinite Atonement, we can change, repent, and move forward into a new future. Bad people can become good, and good people can become better.[1] We can become new creatures in Christ.

That is the central message of the gospel, the doctrine of salvation, the whole point and purpose of life: to change, to become different, and to walk in newness of life (see Romans 6:4). In fact, it could be argued that this sublime truth *is* the gospel—the "good news" that Jesus Christ came to proclaim and of which every prophet before and after Him has borne witness.

When John the Baptist was preaching in the wilderness, preparing the hearts of the people to receive the Messiah, he quoted this passage from the writings of Isaiah: "Every valley shall be filled, and every mountain and hill shall be brought low; and the crooked shall be made straight, and the rough ways shall be made smooth" (Luke 3:5; see also Isaiah 40:4).

Why this passage? What do valleys and mountains have to do with the Savior's impending ministry and Atonement? It seems unlikely that John was talking only about geography or topography. Perhaps these metaphors tell us more about Jesus's mission than we might realize. It's as if he were saying, "Change is coming. Think of something that seems permanent to you—like a mountain. That mountain can be flattened. That's the degree of change that is possible through the gospel of Jesus Christ. Are there things in your life that seem insurmountable? They can be made possible. Does your life seem rough or unstable? Through the Atonement of Jesus Christ, all of that can be made smooth. Anything can change. *You* can change."

While life may be unpredictable and even unfair at times, Jesus Christ came to set it all right. Though you may have made mistakes that took you down a path you did not intend, Jesus Christ came to straighten it all out. He came to change things: darkness to light, evil to goodness, sickness to health, sorrow to joy, despair to hope. Promises of change permeate the scriptures. Through Christ, sins that are red as blood can become white as snow (see Isaiah 1:18); death can lead to new life (see John 11:25–26); captives can be delivered (see Luke 4:18); the blind can see, and the deaf can hear (see Mosiah 3:5); those who mourn can be comforted (see Matthew 5:4); those who hunger and thirst can be filled (see Matthew 5:6); the meek can be exalted and the proud made low (see Matthew 23:12).

So many aspects of Christ's mortal ministry reinforce the concept of second chances. Every time He healed someone who was lame or leprous, for example, not only was He giving that person a second chance at life but He was also teaching us about His ability to heal us spiritually. Consider the man sick with palsy, whose friends lowered him through the roof of the house where Jesus was, in hopes that the Savior would heal him. Obvious to everyone was the man's physical ailment, but clear only to the Savior were his spiritual needs, and those were what He chose to address first. "Son, thy sins be forgiven thee," He said, to the disturbance of the observing Pharisees, who immediately accused Jesus of blasphemy. The Master's response revealed one of His purposes in healing the sick: "That ye may know that the Son of man hath power on earth to forgive sins, . . . I say unto thee, Arise, and take up thy bed, and go thy way" (Mark 2:5–11).

Of course the Savior was interested in alleviating physical suffering, but He knew well that this was not His greatest power or most important mission. What He wanted most was to offer spiritual second chances, new life, and He saw acts of physical healing as a way to impress upon our minds that He has power to heal us spiritually. All such miracles were tangible symbols—adapted to the needs of concrete, finite minds—of deeper, more transcendent spiritual truths.

Everything the Savior said or did—all of the changes He wrought—leads to the most important one of all: the change that occurs in a human soul when he "putteth off the natural man and becometh a saint" (Mosiah 3:19).

An Elemental Part of the Father's Plan

It's easy to see why second chances were such an important part of Christ's message and mission. Our need for second chances was the reason that mission was needed in the first place. Heavenly Father knew from the beginning that sending His children into mortality surrounded by opposition meant that we would slip up, fall, and sometimes fail to get it right. But He bids us to take this walk anyway, knowing that it is the only way we can continue to progress and ultimately become like Him.

It was never part of God's plan that we would stay the same. Adam and Eve needed to leave the Garden of Eden, because if they didn't, "all things which were created must have remained in the same state in which they were after they were created" (2 Nephi 2:22). And that would thwart God's plan, the entire objective of which is that we learn and grow and progress.

The alternative was Satan's perversion of the plan. He wanted to ensure that no one would ever slip up, that no second chance would be needed. Preventing us from making mistakes was Satan's attempt to hold us back and keep us in subjection to him. By accepting the Father's plan and rejecting Lucifer's, we accepted both the possibility that we would falter and the promise that we would receive second chances here on earth.

So that's the pattern. Our relationship with God is one of separation and restoration, of estrangement and reconciliation, of wandering and returning, of picking ourselves up where and when we have fallen, accepting the heavenly second chance, and trying again to live in harmony with higher ideals rather than with our lower impulses. Our loving Father's mercy knows no bounds, His compassion no limits, His love no end. He sent His Only Begotten Son to live and die for us and, ultimately, to give us another chance.

"Recalculating"

Doesn't this tell us something about how we should view our mistakes? Are our expectations so high that we forget the bigger picture—God's bigger picture—and refuse to give ourselves and others a second chance? The Lord's perspective is defined by understanding, patience, love, and hope. Always hope. He knows that, just like the barren ivy and brown grass and dormant bulbs, life can be renewed and hope reborn in any moment. But do *we* know it? Or do we expect perfection in spiritual matters? Do we chastise ourselves and never forgive our sins and shortcomings, large or small? Do we want so much to get it right the first time that we are paralyzed by our fears and doubts?

The purpose of life is to be tutored, to make course corrections, to repent, and to get back more fully on the gospel path in following the Lord. Speaking of heaven, our postmortal estate, President Dieter F. Uchtdorf said, "Remember: the heavens will not be filled with those who never made mistakes but with those who recognized that they were off course and who corrected their ways to get back in the light of gospel truth."[2] And we do that throughout life.

Think how much better we would fare if we had more of an attitude of learning and moving on from setbacks and mistakes than being defined or paralyzed by them. I like how Emily Watts compares the matter-of-fact tone of a GPS to an ideal attitude toward accepting course corrections in life. "Here's what I really love about the GPS," she says. "When you miss the turn, it doesn't fall apart. It just calmly says, 'Recalculating,' and tells you how to fix your mistake." And then she laments, "I wish I could be as gentle and objective about my life mistakes as the GPS is about my driving ones."[3] What a crucial insight! Once we come to see mistakes as building blocks for a better life rather than stumbling blocks that keep us down, we truly begin to understand the gospel of second chances.

Of course, our Heavenly Father would prefer that we not commit sin in the first place, and the scriptures contain many warnings against seeking happiness in wickedness (see Alma 41:10; Helaman 13:38; Mormon 2:13; Isaiah 57:21; Psalm 32:10).

But He also knew that we would make mistakes, and we would need a Savior. He knows how great the distance is between where we are and where He is, and for that reason, He wants us not only to believe in second chances but also to seek for them.

If we're striving toward a good and righteous life, we're on our way. We're on the path and headed in the right direction. We stumble and fall now and then, but we get up and we learn and we keep moving forward with our Lord's divine assistance. As the Savior urged His disciples at the Last Supper, "Let not your heart be troubled, neither let it be afraid" (John 14:27).

CHAPTER 3

GOD WANTS US TO BELIEVE IN SECOND CHANCES

These are written, that ye might believe that Jesus is the Christ, the Son of God; and that believing ye might have life through his name.

JOHN 20:31

As soon as we begin to look for examples of second chances in life, we see them everywhere. We observe both well-known and lesser-known people who struggle for a time and then find success and happiness later in life. We encounter businesses that struggle but then are reborn through new leadership, products, innovations, and strategic planning. We see people with dim diagnoses of health who somehow get a new lease on life. We rejoice over children who are adopted into loving families. We know of students who struggle in school and yet, in time, become accomplished contributors to society. We witness prodigal adolescents and adults who come to themselves and return from far countries and riotous living to change their lives and begin again (see Luke 15:11–32).

Of course, the opposite is also true. People once vibrant and strong can become desolate and weak. But even in those cases, there is always the hope of change, renewal, and rebirth. The cycles and seasons of life are never ending.

Is there something in our spiritual subconscious that attracts us to stories of second chances? Is it reasonable to expect that the Light of Christ, which is given to every mortal soul, would inspire in everyone a longing to believe that second chances are possible? Could this be why the concept of second chances is a theme as old as time, and abundant in scripture, literature, history, and our own experience?

EXAMPLES IN THE BOOK OF MORMON

Not surprisingly, the best place to find stories of second chances is in the scriptures. When we read through the lens of second chances, we see this theme throughout holy writ. We don't have to read very far in the Book of Mormon before coming upon the story of Nephi and his brothers trying and failing to obtain the plates of brass from Laban and then trying and failing again before finally succeeding (see 1 Nephi 3–4). And that's just the first example.

In some ways, the Book of Mormon could be considered a book about second chances. Think about some of the most prominent figures in the Book of Mormon, those whose teachings and valiant acts are most inspiring to us. It's interesting to note how many of them needed a second chance.

Take Alma, for example. He was part of a group of wicked priests serving in the court of a wicked king when the prophet Abinadi came preaching repentance (see Mosiah 11). Alma alone believed and defended Abinadi, repented of his sins, and established the church among his small group of Nephites (see Mosiah 17–18). Because he was given a second chance, he eventually became the spiritual leader of the entire Nephite nation and received from the Lord the promise of eternal life (see Mosiah 26:8, 20).

Alma's son Alma went through an even more dramatic transformation. He spent years trying to destroy the church his father had established—no doubt breaking his father's heart—before he got his second chance and later succeeded his father as the presiding high priest (see Mosiah 27; 29:42). Some of the richest, most inspiring doctrinal sermons in all of scripture on such topics as conversion (see Alma 5), faith (see Alma 32), the resurrection (see Alma 40–41), and justice and mercy (see Alma 42) came from this man who needed and accepted a second chance.

One of Alma's fields of labor was also given a second chance. When he first entered Ammonihah to preach, he was spat upon and cast out of the city. Weighed down with sorrow over the wickedness of the city's inhabitants, Alma was ready to take his message elsewhere. Then an angel stopped him and told him to go back to Ammonihah—to give the people another chance to accept the word of God. Tellingly, Alma "returned speedily" (Alma 8:18). Even though he had just been rejected and abused, he trusted the Lord and reentered the city by another way.

Even on his second attempt, Alma did not seem to have much success. In fact, he and his companion, Amulek, were forced to witness the martyrdom of women and children who believed in the word of God (see Alma 14). But he did find Amulek, and he did witness the dramatic conversion of the lawyer Zeezrom, who fled Ammonihah with a handful of believers. Of all people, Alma, whose father was converted by a prophet whose efforts appeared to have failed, could understand the lengths to which Heavenly Father will go to offer even one of His children a second chance.

Alma's cohorts during his wayward years—Ammon, Aaron, Omner, and Himni—all underwent a transformation similar to Alma's and then embarked on one of the most successful missionary endeavors in history. Their second chance led directly to the conversion of "many" (Alma 17:4), including the king of all the Lamanites (see Alma 17–27).

The Lamanites taught by Ammon and his brothers were notoriously idle and bloodthirsty, but once the Atonement had a chance to work in their hearts, they became "distinguished for their zeal towards God, and also towards men" (Alma 27:27). Their transformation was so complete, in fact, that they buried their weapons during a time of war, because "rather than shed the blood of their brethren they would give up their own lives" (Alma 24:18). In a larger sense, this mass conversion of Lamanites could be seen as a second chance extended to the descendants of Laman and Lemuel, who had been cursed and cut off because of their rebellion but who had never been left without the hope that repentance could restore them to the fold of God.[1] The Nephites also benefited from this second chance, because it produced the sons of Helaman, the Lamanite stripling warriors, who volunteered to assist the Nephites in battle and who probably saved the Nephites from destruction at the hands of their enemies.

The list goes on and on. There's a telling passage in the Book of Mormon that lists the names of those Alma had chosen to accompany him on an important mission to preach the gospel to a group of apostates (see Alma 31:32). The list includes Ammon, Aaron, and Omner, who were now several years removed from their rebellious days; Amulek, who had once described himself as one who "was called many times and . . . would not hear," who "went on rebelling against God" (Alma 10:6); and Zeezrom, who had offered Amulek money if he would deny God but then experienced a mighty change of his own. In other words, Alma's missionary team was composed of people who were currently enjoying their second chance.

If you ever wonder whether you are so deep in sin that you are beyond hope, that God could no longer have any possible use for you, there is no better place to utterly refute those doubts than in the Book of Mormon. Or if your heart ever groans, as Nephi's did, because, despite your best efforts, temptations and sins seem to "so easily beset [you]" (2 Nephi 4:18), there is no better place to find hope and encouragement than in the Book of Mormon. The overwhelming message of the book is that people can change, that the Atonement of Jesus Christ can reach everyone, even "the very vilest of sinners" (Mosiah 28:4), and turn them into "instruments in the hands of God" (Mosiah 27:36). It's as if the Book of Mormon is saying to us, "If a second chance can come to Alma, Ammon, Zeezrom, and King Lamoni, then it can certainly come to you."

As the title page declares, the purpose of the Book of Mormon is to convince everyone "that Jesus is the Christ," and what better way to do that than to compile example upon example of people who repented and partook of the Savior's Atonement—some in impressive, dramatic fashion and others in more gradual, subtle ways. If the central message of the gospel truly is that we can change, then perhaps this significant emphasis on repentance is one reason the Lord has said that the Book of Mormon contains "the fulness of the gospel of Jesus Christ" (D&C 20:9). One simply cannot read the Book of Mormon and after reaching the end of it still wonder whether someone who has sinned can have a second chance.

And that's just the Book of Mormon!

Examples in the Bible

Examples of second chances abound in the other volumes of scripture as well. Remember Joseph, who was sold as a slave into Egypt by his brothers? Envious of Joseph's favored status with their father, Jacob, Joseph's brothers staged his death and sent Jacob into deep mourning. Several years later, in the midst of widespread famine, Joseph had been placed in charge of Egypt's food storage program when his brothers came desperately seeking food. They didn't recognize their brother, but he recognized them and decided to test them. He framed Benjamin, the youngest and their father's other favorite, and accused him of theft. He said he would allow the others to return home but demanded that Benjamin remain to be punished for his crime.

Isn't that a cruel, vengeful trick? Perhaps it seems that way, but in reality it was a merciful offer of a second chance. Joseph was giving his brothers the opportunity to right their wrong and prove they had changed. They passed the test, refusing to abandon their brother Benjamin as they had their brother Joseph those many years before. Once Joseph saw how they handled their second chance, he was overcome with emotion and tearfully revealed himself to them, even forgiving their former cruelty, saying, "Now therefore be not grieved, nor angry with yourselves, that ye sold me hither: for God did send me before you to preserve life" (Genesis 45:5).

Jonah's second chance is another memorable example. Called to cry repentance to the people of Nineveh, Jonah refused—perhaps out of fear, perhaps out of prejudice against a heathen people—and ran away from his assignment. The Lord, of course, wouldn't give up on Jonah as easily as Jonah seemed willing to give up on Nineveh. Why did He give Jonah a second chance to fulfill his appointed mission? Wouldn't it have been less trouble to find someone else to preach to the people of Nineveh? The fact is that second chances are part of His plan. He knows that we don't always do the right thing the first time, and He has accounted for that. Concerning Jonah and his second chance, Elder Juan Uceda of the Seventy wrote: "It is comforting to know that we worship a God who is merciful and who allows His children many chances to learn His ways and be obedient to them. Who among us would be saved without a second chance—more than one opportunity to prove ourselves in the sight of God?"[2]

Even some of the Bible's spiritual giants grew to their stature after being given a second chance. Simon Peter, whose name given him by the Lord meant "a stone" (John 1:42), proved to be less solid than he thought he was during his moment of intense trial, denying three times that he knew the Savior (see Luke

22:55–62). But Jesus saw Peter—as He often sees all of us—for what he could be, not for what he was. When given a second chance to prove his faithfulness, Peter showed that he was every bit a rock, as solid as the Lord knew he could be. Peter led the Church after Christ's Ascension and eventually gave his life for the gospel.

Perhaps the most prominent example of second chances in scripture is the one given to the Apostle Paul. Once known for his zeal in persecuting Christians, Paul was equally zealous in promoting the cause of Christ once he learned the truth. On that road to Damascus, a radical shift occurred in his life when he received the grace of God. After his encounter with the risen Lord, a mighty change happened in his heart and mind (see Acts 9). Instead of seeking to destroy Christians out of his hatred, he worked to bless and build them up out of his consuming love. The greatest of sinners became the greatest of Saints, who came to know that "the goodness of God leadeth . . . to repentance" (Romans 2:4). Paul will forever stand as an example of one who was willing to admit his mistakes and take full advantage of the second chance he was given.

Examples in Church History

Examples of second chances are not limited to ancient scripture. In more modern times, we have the example of Martin Harris and Joseph Smith and the loss of 116 manuscript pages of the Book of Mormon. Indeed, the story reveals much about how the gospel of second chances operates. Neither Joseph Smith nor Martin Harris could reclaim the lost pages. They were lost—gone! Joseph wrote that he "suffered temporally as well as spiritually" for the loss. He also wrote that he "was chastened" and the plates were "taken from [him] for a season."[3]

But the Lord knew that would happen, and He had prepared a way to compensate for the mortal frailties of His servants. Centuries before, He instructed Mormon, as he compiled the Book of Mormon record, to include plates that amounted to a duplicate of the first part of the book. These plates, the small plates of Nephi, today replace the 116 lost pages. No, Joseph and Martin could not reclaim what was lost, and they could not go back and undo what they had done. But because of the Lord's mercy and goodness, everything worked out, and each was given a second chance. Martin Harris, after a period of sincere repentance, was chosen to be one of the Three Witnesses to the Book of Mormon. Joseph Smith, after his own repentance, received the plates again and was allowed to translate, with this assurance from the Lord: "Thou art still chosen, and art again called to the work" (D&C 3:10). Both Martin and Joseph came out of the experience wiser, humbler, and more committed to "seek not to counsel the Lord, but to take counsel from his hand" (Jacob 4:10).

The experience of Oliver Granger, another example from Church history, also helps us understand that the Lord is patient with us and offers us the opportunity to get up and try again. "Oliver Granger was a very ordinary man," President Boyd K. Packer noted. "He was mostly blind having 'lost his sight by cold and exposure' (*History of the Church,* 4:408). The First Presidency described him as 'a man of the most strict integrity and moral virtue; and in fine, to be a man of God' (*History of the Church,*

3:350)." Oliver Granger was the Prophet Joseph's agent for the Church when the Saints left Kirtland and then again when they left Independence, Far West, and Nauvoo. He stayed behind for a time to sell whatever properties he could for what little he could. He never really had much success, but the Lord honored him for trying—and then trying again. "Let him contend earnestly for the redemption of the First Presidency of my Church," the Lord said. "And when he falls he shall rise again, for his sacrifice shall be more sacred unto me than his increase" (D&C 117:13). "What did Oliver Granger do that his name should be held in sacred remembrance?" President Packer asked. "Nothing much, really. *It was not so much what he did as what he was.*"[4]

Although Oliver Granger did not gain much financially for the Church, his efforts were not in vain. His experience of falling and rising again was important—even sacred—to the Lord. It shows that character is not a result of a perfect or "successful" life, not a product of never having made a mistake or an error of judgment but rather of getting back up after we have fallen. Character comes of rising again in unwavering righteousness and of trusting in the Lord.

President Packer continued: "Some worry endlessly over missions that were missed, or marriages that did not turn out, or babies that did not arrive, or children that seem lost, or dreams unfulfilled, or because age limits what they can do. I do not think it pleases the Lord when we worry because we think we never do enough or that what we do is never good enough.

"Some needlessly carry a heavy burden of guilt which could be removed through confession and repentance.

"The Lord did not say of Oliver, '[*If*] he falls,' but '*When* he falls he shall rise again' (D&C 117:13; emphasis added)."[5]

Think of the hope in that statement! The Lord knows we will falter and make mistakes, but it does not keep Him from asking us to do His work. With each stumble comes the choice of getting up again—or staying down. The Lord loves and honors our efforts, our sacrifices, even "more . . . than [our] increase" (D&C 117:13). We worship a God who is longsuffering and patient, a God who truly knows our heart and our desires, a God who gives us the opportunity to get up and dust ourselves off whenever we fall.

EXAMPLES IN THE WORLD AROUND US

It seems clear from the sheer volume of scriptural examples that God wants us to believe in second chances. But holy writ is not the only way He tries to communicate with His children. The world He created for us—His handiwork—is full of signs and symbols and reminders that no disaster is permanent and that second chances are possible.

The regular pattern of the seasons is a good example. Every spring brings the promise of a new beginning. No matter how miserably last year's harvest may have failed, the next spring offers the opportunity to replant and try again. No matter how bleak and cold the winter may be, we always know, without the slightest doubt, that the world will be warmed and renewed with the coming of spring. It happens every year. We never think to ourselves, "I know spring has always come in the past, but this winter has been so harsh and difficult that spring can't possibly come this time. I'm just sure it will stay winter forever." Why, then, do we think that about the winters of our lives? Why do we ever doubt the possibility of a second chance?

I believe symbols of second chances are all around us. Every morning's sunrise is God's daily reminder to us that new beginnings and second chances are possible—a reminder that light will always come to dispel darkness and that each new day can be a fresh start, a new opportunity to do a little better than we did yesterday. Is it unreasonable to think that Heavenly Father planned things this way to encourage us to seek for second chances and accept opportunities for them?

Even our physical bodies can be seen as living symbols of the gospel of second chances. A doctor does remarkably little to heal a broken bone. In most cases, he or she will simply look at the X-ray, make sure the bones are properly aligned, stabilize the fracture, and tell the patient to wait a few weeks. The body does the actual healing all by itself.

After most of our minor injuries, and even some major ones, the miraculous bodies God created give us second chances. No matter how the injury happened, whether it was a result of our own foolishness or simply an accident or an ailment, in time, we are most often restored to good health, as if nothing had ever happened!

Perhaps because these symbols and reminders are so commonplace, we may not always recognize or appreciate them. But as soon as we open our eyes to evidence of second chances around us, it's easy to see that God wants us to believe that second chances are possible.

CHAPTER 4

SECOND CHANCES ARE FOR EVERYONE

There is never a time when the spirit is too old to approach God.
All are within the reach of pardoning mercy.

JOSEPH SMITH

Not long ago, a man I know was caught in a web of lies and moral deceit. For some time, he had lived a double life—seemingly devout and committed to the gospel while at home with his wife and children, but while away on frequent business trips, he engaged in serious immorality. As a consequence, he lost his membership in the Church and began a difficult repentance process.

This man is essentially good. He and his loving wife have raised an exemplary family. They blessed many lives as they served faithfully in the Church. But here a little, there a little, incrementally and over time, he veered off course so that his life slowly and subtly descended into sin and duplicity until finally he sank so low as to break solemn covenants and the tender hearts of his loved ones. In the depths of self-betrayal, he deceived himself, his family, ward and stake members, and neighbors—but not the Lord.

For several years, my friend's life was very different from what his family thought it was. As a result, it became very different from what he had dreamed it would be. He sat outside the temple, heartbroken that he could not enter to see his daughter get married. He was unable to ordain his son an elder and send him into the mission field with the example and blessing of a worthy father emblazoned in his heart. His soul was racked with torment, and he felt such abject despair and hopelessness that, at times, he did not know if he could see it through. The process of repentance was deep and difficult.

Years of heartfelt repentance have changed this man. He is now in full fellowship in the Church. He holds his wife's hand a little tighter now. His prayers are deeper, his self-awareness clearer. He knows his weak spots and vulnerabilities. He knows the edges of dangerous cliffs from which he must stay far away, and he now guards against iniquity more carefully. He knows that his godly sorrow will be forever written on his heart. But he also knows that he is clean, he has been forgiven, and the Lord loves him.

He said to me, "I know the Atonement is real. It's not just a scriptural concept or nice thought for me. It's not just a Sunday School lesson anymore. It's *real.* Without the hope of the gospel and the reality of the Savior's Atonement, His love and forgiveness, I would have given up long ago. I *know* the Atonement is real. I have experienced its anguish and its joy." He spoke humbly of walking a lonely path, of the profound hurt and pain he caused, of reestablishing trust and respect in those he loves. He knows in the deepest part of his soul that he has been given another chance. It is not too late for his life to end well.

This story—and many others like it—illustrates the depth and reach of Christ's atoning power. It is a reminder that even grievous sin and years of deception can be overcome and washed clean. While most of us have not and probably never will do anything quite so serious, we may have friends or family members who have fallen into transgression that puts their Church membership in jeopardy.

There are advantages and disadvantages, when teaching and learning about the Atonement, of focusing on examples involving grievous sin. One advantage is that such examples are impressive and memorable. Another is that they testify of the breadth and depth of the Atonement. They show that no one has fallen so far that the Savior cannot reach them.

But if we do not also learn of the power of the Atonement to help us make our course corrections, then we're missing much of the Atonement's daily relevance and power. This would be a potentially damning mistake.

To use an analogy that may be somewhat imperfect, if the price of admission to the circus is $5, it doesn't matter whether you have 5 cents or $4.99—they're not going to let you in unless you have $5. Spiritually speaking, the "price of admission" was described by the Lord Himself: "No unclean thing can enter into his kingdom." And none of us can afford that price unless we have "washed [our] garments in [His] blood, because of [our] faith, and the repentance of all [our] sins, and [our] faithfulness unto the end" (3 Nephi 27:19).

A related mistake is to assume that only those who have committed serious sins can fully appreciate the Atonement. It's true that, in my friend's case, the Atonement became more real to him because of the intensity of the repentance he went through. But I believe that those who remain close to the Spirit are more likely, not less, to understand the unfathomable value of what Christ did for us—such things, after all, can be understood only through the Holy Ghost, and the Holy Ghost will not dwell in unclean tabernacles.[1]

In other words, we need not be guilty of serious sin in order to need, to appreciate, and to take advantage of a second chance. In fact, sometimes we may find ourselves hoping for a second chance that has nothing to do with sin at all. How many times have we made innocent mistakes—not out of rebellion but just out of ignorance or poor judgment—and wished we could try again? How often has a misunderstanding led to a strained relationship, and we wished we could go back in time to do things differently?

Fractured Relationships

Recently, a good woman whom we will call Naomi shared how she was given a second chance to mend a relationship. Another woman in Naomi's ward (whom we will call Cathy) had been unkind to her and ostracized her, claiming that her son had been mistreated by Naomi's son. As much as Naomi and her son tried to patch things up and despite the fact that her accusations were false, Cathy continued to snub Naomi. Of course, apologies were offered and behavior was monitored, but to no avail. The offended woman remained offended. Naomi worried and prayed over the situation. She did not know how to make it better. She prayed for a second chance.

One day Naomi went to the temple with this problem weighing on her mind and heart. She put Cathy's name on the temple prayer roll. Naomi felt that she had tried everything she could think of to make amends. Not thirty minutes after Naomi returned from the temple, she received a phone call from her ward Relief Society president, asking if she would be Cathy's visiting teaching partner. Naomi explained the rift in their relationship to the Relief Society president and wondered if she should rethink her request.

After some pondering, the wise Relief Society president recommended that Naomi proceed with the assignment as if nothing were wrong. Apprehensive, Naomi called Cathy, even though the two had not spoken to each other in quite some time. And then the miracle happened. As they talked about their assignment, the distance between them began to fade.

Naomi and Cathy never discussed the situation that had caused their estrangement. Somehow they did not need to. Their hearts were healed as they served together as representatives of Jesus Christ to other women in their ward. They knew there was no place for animosity or hurt feelings. They both received a second chance as they looked to the Lord and sought to do His will.

Sometime later, the Relief Society president followed up with Naomi and asked how her relationship with Cathy was progressing. Naomi thanked the Relief Society president for being in tune with the Spirit of the Lord and for affording her the opportunity for things to be made right with Cathy.

LIFE'S RANDOM "FALLENNESS"

Naomi hadn't done anything sinful that caused her to want a second chance with Cathy. In a sense, she had simply experienced some of what we could call life's random "fallenness." The fact is, we live in an imperfect world, where imperfect things happen to imperfect people. That's part of what we signed up for when we chose to come into mortality—it's part of the journey and test of life to see how we'll handle life's arbitrary ironies and difficulties.

Anyone who has lived even a few years knows that mortality is full of twists and turns, triumphs and letdowns, setbacks and successes. In our mind's eye, we have a plan for our lives and the lives of our children. Then *life* happens. We mess up, make mistakes, fumble, and falter; *they* mess up, make mistakes, fumble, and falter. We face opposition, encounter difficulty and disappointment, and experience much of sorrow and heartache. The great message of Jesus Christ and His redeeming grace is that things don't have to stay that way. Through the Atonement we can overcome all of it—yes, even random accidents and tribulations that are not violations of eternal law, though they may be violations of personal comfort. I'm speaking not of the cleansing power of the Atonement but rather of its strengthening, uplifting power. Here is an example:

We have some wonderful neighbors whose house burned to the ground some years ago. Virtually in an instant, essentially everything was gone. I saw them step up, muster their courage, and put into practice the principles of faith, hope, and perseverance that they had believed and taught. In a real sense, they were starting over. The wife said to me, "When we were married forty years ago, we started out with nothing. We can do it again."

She told me that the experience helped reaffirm to her that it was all just "stuff" and that they were blessed to still have their family, their relationships, and their testimonies. They may have been without a house for a season, but they did not lose their home, because while their house was built of flammable things, their home was built on eternal things: love, righteousness, and sacred covenants.

Through resolute faith, prayers, and the support of many people who love them (and fire insurance!), they have rebuilt their house and their lives. It hasn't been easy. It's been a long, sometimes very difficult road. But when asked how his wife was coping with the heartache, the husband responded, "It's her finest hour."

The fire, which could have destroyed them, changed them for the better. It gave them an opportunity for a second chance at life—a new beginning. They experienced for themselves the prophetic and reassuring words of Isaiah when he spoke of "beauty for ashes, the oil of joy for mourning, the garment of praise for the spirit of heaviness" (Isaiah 61:3).

I don't know whether a devastating house fire was part of Heavenly Father's plan for this couple. But I do know that living in a fallen world, where misfortune, heartache, suffering, and difficulty happen, is part of His plan for all of us. And another part of His plan is the atoning grace of His Son, which helps us overcome it.

I am so grateful for this truth about the Atonement: When Christ suffered for us, He took upon Himself not only our sins but also our pains, sicknesses, heartaches, and afflictions. In Alma 7 we learn how and why the Savior is able to provide this enabling power:

"He shall go forth, suffering pains and afflictions and temptations of every kind; and this that the word might be fulfilled which saith he will take upon him the pains and the sicknesses of his people. And he will take upon him death, that he may loose the bands of death which bind his people; and he will take upon him their infirmities, that his bowels may be filled with mercy, according to the flesh, that he may know according to the flesh how to succor his people according to their infirmities" (Alma 7:11–12).

"The Savior has suffered not just for our iniquities but also for the inequality, the unfairness, the pain, the anguish, and the emotional distresses that so frequently beset us," said Elder David A. Bednar. "There is no physical pain, no anguish of soul, no suffering of spirit, no infirmity or weakness that you or I ever experience during our mortal journey that the Savior did not experience first. You and I in a moment of weakness may cry out, 'No one understands. No one knows.' No human being, perhaps, knows. But the Son of God perfectly knows and understands, for He felt and bore our burdens before we ever did. And because He paid the ultimate price and bore that burden, He has perfect empathy and can extend to us His arm of mercy in so many phases of our life. He can reach out, touch, succor—literally run to us—and strengthen us to be more than we could ever be and help us to do that which we could never do through relying upon only our own power."[2] Our Redeemer will redeem us; our Savior will save us from the vicissitudes and heartaches of this life. He who knows and understands all things will help us with *all* things.

The Savior chose to pay the price of our sins because that was necessary to reconcile us to the Father. He chose to suffer our pain because He loves us and wanted to put Himself in the best position possible to strengthen and succor us.

CHRIST'S ATONEMENT COVERS IT ALL

Because of the hope and power of the Atonement of Jesus Christ, tragedy can become triumph, and failure can be the prelude to success. In fact, sometimes the failure or setback serves as a stepping-stone to something even greater. Our friends who lost their house eventually rebuilt, and they developed spiritual qualities that might have remained hidden had it not been for their tragedy. My friend who repented of moral transgression will never be able to make up for the time he lost while living a double life, but he is now back in full fellowship, and the Savior's grace is turning his weaknesses into strengths (see Ether 12:27).

Grace—which is at the heart of all second chances—is a gift from God. It is unearned divine assistance, unmerited divine favor, divine enabling power to accomplish things that could never otherwise be accomplished. God's grace is His tender mercy and goodwill, His continuous love and compassion, His condescension toward the children of men.[3] Fortunately, the Lord's saving grace can apply to all situations and all circumstances. All types of second chances come because of Christ. When He invites those who are "heavy laden" to come unto Him, He's not just talking about those laden with sin (Matthew 11:28). The Lord will give us all the strength, all the courage, all the faith and hope we need to rebuild and go on with our lives, no matter what happened. That is the miracle of a second chance.

CHAPTER 5

ACKNOWLEDGING THE NEED TO CHANGE

Search me, O God, and know my heart:
try me, and know my thoughts:
And see if there be any wicked way in me,
and lead me in the way everlasting.

PSALM 139:23–24

Sometimes it seems much easier to talk about second chances than it is to actually experience one. The trouble is that as much as God wants us to believe in second chances, Satan does not. And one of his most effective deceptions is to convince basically good people that they do not need a second chance. "All is well," he tells them. "You're fine. Your sins, if you have any, are small compared to those of other people. Don't worry about it. All is well." In this way, he blinds their hearts, and they become their own great barrier to repentance.

At one time or another, we are all subject to that kind of deception. In a way, we are like my daughter who, at the age of five, insisted that she did not need glasses, even though an eye exam indicated otherwise. "I can see!" she protested. And she could, but not as well as she would when fitted with her first pair of glasses. Slowly, carefully, she rested the glasses on her nose and opened her eyes to a whole new world. She saw details she'd never seen before: the veins on leaves, the pockmarks in brick, the pointed grass blades that had been blurred. She literally had her eyes opened, and now that she could truly see, she rejoiced in her newfound vision!

Who, through life experience and the process of maturity, hasn't had his or her eyes opened? Do we ever really know how blind we have been until after we are able to finally see?

If we are teachable, if we are humble and meek, if we submissively turn to the Lord, we can create a new life—one that we didn't even realize was available to us. If we don't dig in our heels when we make mistakes, God can use us again. If we receive the Lord's guidance and correction when we stray, He can make us better, stronger, wiser, more empathetic, and softhearted. God's grace can transform our setbacks and stumbles into a prelude for a great second act in life. God can turn the bitter into sweet, the ugly into beauty.

THE EXAMPLE OF JOHN NEWTON

Years before he penned the now-famous words "I once was lost but now am found, was blind but now I see," John Newton was a slave trader with little use for religion. His upbringing did not include much spiritual instruction after his mother died, and his many years at sea introduced him to what he called "profane practices,"[1] in which he indulged liberally. Life as a sailor got so bad for Newton that he later admitted that the only reason he didn't commit suicide was because he wanted to murder his captain first.

But then a violent storm at sea finally brought him face to face with his own mortality and turned his thoughts toward God, whom he had long since abandoned. Although he was sure he was beyond forgiveness and frankly still doubted whether the Bible was even true, yet he started reading the New Testament and examining his life. He finally determined to give Christianity—and himself—a second chance.

Interestingly, however, John Newton's spiritual awakening did not inspire him right away to get out of the slave-trading business. Even after becoming an ordained minister with a large following, he continued to invest money in the slave trade. As easy as it is for us, hundreds of years later, to see the moral contradiction in a Christian preacher selling men and women into slavery, that contradiction long remained a blind spot in John Newton. Despite all of the meaningful reforms he had made to his life, he did not yet see the need to change his slave-trading ways.

Fortunately, John Newton, though once blind, did eventually see. Before the end of his life, he wrote an influential publication denouncing slavery and confessing his shame at ever having been involved in it. He also became a powerful supporter of William Wilberforce, the member of Parliament who led the fight to abolish slavery in Great Britain.[2]

John Newton wrote, "We think we know a great deal, because we are ignorant of what remains to be learnt."[3] His life exemplifies that truth. The more we improve our lives, the more we see our need to improve even further. The more we recognize our own blindness, the more we are able to see.

Perhaps that's why John Newton's song "Amazing Grace" is the most recorded song on the planet and one of the most beloved. It offers hope to those grieving or lost or searching for meaning in life. Some have even suggested that this song about second chances may be one of the theme songs in heaven. Its simple melody and message reverberate in our souls:

> *Amazing Grace, how sweet the sound,*
> *That saved a wretch like me.*
> *I once was lost but now am found,*
> *Was blind, but now I see.*
>
> *'Twas Grace that taught my heart to fear.*
> *And Grace, my fears relieved.*
> *How precious did that Grace appear*
> *The hour I first believed.*
>
> *Through many dangers, toils and snares*
> *I have already come;*
> *'Tis Grace that brought me safe thus far*
> *And Grace will lead me home.* [4]

Except for our perfect Savior, we have all made mistakes. We've all had to face unfortunate and challenging circumstances, and hopefully, we have all come to realize that we can improve our vision. We may not be seeing things as they really are or as the Lord would really like them to be. We've all come up short from time to time, and we'll continue to do so throughout mortality.

In fact, I'm certain you could follow any gospel teacher or writer with a hidden camera for a few weeks, and you would discover some less-than-perfect moments in his or her life. No one, *no one,* is perfect or infallible. That's not to say that we're all hypocrites,[5] but it is to say that we "all have sinned, and come short of the glory of God" (Romans 3:23).[6]

We all fall short of the ideal for our personal lives and relationships, our work and Church callings, our spending and financial decisions, and our relationship with God. The truth is that "people are sinful, they stray, they often avoid what is elevating and yearn for that which is despicable. If they are devoid of divine aid and without spiritual resuscitation, they remain forever lost and fallen (1 Ne. 10:6), enemies to God and to themselves (Mosiah 3:19; Alma 41:11), spiritually stillborn."[7]

Few doctrines receive a stronger confirmation in daily life than the Fall. Our fallen world is beset by sin and temptation, filled with the fleshly susceptibilities of natural men and women, and so the question is not whether we will trip and fall, falter and stumble, but rather how we will respond when we do. Will we pick ourselves up, dust ourselves off, and try again? Or will we give in to despair and disillusionment? Will we recognize our need for the Savior, for renewal and redemption from this fallen state, or will we surrender to the pull of the world and the allurements of the adversary?

Elder Bruce C. Hafen put it this way: "If you have problems in your life, don't assume there is something wrong with you. Struggling with those problems is at the very core of life's purpose. As we draw close to God, He will show us our weaknesses and through them make us wiser, stronger. If you're seeing more of your weaknesses, that just might mean you're moving nearer to God, not farther away."[8]

Two Lessons from Oliver Cromwell's Warts

The story is told that when Oliver Cromwell, English statesman and Lord Protector of England, first saw the portrait for which he had posed, he took offense and insisted that it be repainted. His objection was that the painting portrayed him with a clear and flawless complexion. "Where are the warts?" he asked. The custom at the time was for portrait artists to idealize their subjects, and the artist had been careful to paint an unblemished portrait. Cromwell, however, demanded that his likeness be repainted more realistically, "warts and all."

What are the lessons we can learn from Oliver Cromwell's warts? I believe there are at least two.

For one thing, we all have warts. When confronted with our weaknesses and blemishes, we may be tempted to cover them up, hope that no one notices, blame others, or make excuses. We may not be proud of our weaknesses, but being aware and meek enough to accept responsibility for them is vital to our growth. Someday we hope that those we love will honor our memory and remember how we strove to accept the amazing and healing grace of our Lord Jesus Christ. They may be proud of all the times we were right and of all we accomplished, but they may be even more inspired by the times we admitted we were wrong, the times we stumbled and got back up, the times we realized we were blind but were willing to see that we needed a Savior.

"Repentance is not a negative principle, but rather a positive, most glorious one," wrote Elder Tad R. Callister. "It did not come from an angry, overbearing parent, but from the most loving Father of all. It is not for the wicked alone, but for every good and great person who wants to be better. It is for every individual who has not yet reached perfection."[9] And Elder D. Todd Christofferson memorably taught: "The prophetic call [to repent] should be received with joy. Without repentance, there is no real progress or improvement in life. Pretending there is no sin does not lessen its burden. . . . Repentance is a divine gift, and there should be a smile on our faces when we speak of it."[10] The first step in the direction of perfection is exercising the faith to acknowledge that we're not there yet.

There is another lesson we can learn from the story of Oliver Cromwell's warts: although this great man admirably insisted that his portrait accurately portray reality—warts and all—too much of this attitude could lead us to feel comfortable with or even proud or defensive of our weaknesses. Unfortunately, sometimes phrases like "Nobody's perfect" or "We're only human" are used to justify sinful behavior rather than to encourage humility and repentance.

I wonder if that attitude is at the heart of the false doctrine taught by Nehor, and perpetuated by many others throughout history, "that all mankind should be saved at the last day, and that they need not fear nor tremble, but that they might lift up their heads and rejoice; for the Lord had created all men, and had also redeemed all men; and, in the end, all men should have eternal life" (Alma 1:4). Doesn't that sound remarkably like the plan Satan presented in the Council in Heaven? (see Moses 4:1).

It's a lot like saying, "God couldn't possibly punish you for sinning, because everybody sins. It's part of our nature. So stop worrying. Indulge your natural appetites and desires, and in the end God will change you and make you holy and give you eternal life."[11] No wonder Nehor got rich for teaching such things.

"I Want Present Salvation"

Part of the deviousness of Nehor's philosophy is that it acknowledges that sin is bad and should be corrected—just not right now. It recognizes the need for redemption but relegates it to something that happens "in the end." We hear that sentiment in St. Augustine's plea, "Lord, give me chastity but do not give it yet."

Contrast this perspective with President Brigham Young's statement: "I want present salvation. I preach, comparatively, but little about the eternities and Gods, and their wonderful works in eternity; and do not tell who first made them, nor how they were made; for I know nothing about that. Life is for us, and it is for us to receive it today, and not wait for the millennium. Let us take a course to be saved today, and, when evening comes, review the acts of the day, repent of our sins, if we have any to repent of, and say our prayers; then we can lie down and sleep in peace until the morning, arise with gratitude to God, commence the labors of another day, and strive to live the whole day to God and nobody else."[12]

Consider these words of Amulek, which seem to be a direct

refutation of Nehor's philosophy: "Now is the time and the day of your salvation; and therefore, if ye will repent and harden not your hearts, *immediately* shall the great plan of redemption be brought about unto you" (Alma 34:31; emphasis added; see also vv. 32–37).

If you ever wonder about the daily relevance of the Atonement, remember the account of Peter walking on the water. When he became fearful and began to sink, Peter cried out for the Lord to save him, "and *immediately* Jesus stretched forth his hand, and caught him" (Matthew 14:31; emphasis added). The Lord will be there for us. God's gift of renewal and rebirth, of rescue and hope, of peace and joy can be with us every step of the way—not just on Judgment Day.

It has been wisely noted that having one foot in yesterday and one foot in tomorrow is an unstable position. The best way to face the future, it seems, is to keep both feet in today. We can't spend too much time looking back—or even looking too far ahead, for that matter.

"We do not know when we will be required to leave this mortal existence," said President Thomas S. Monson. "And so [we] ask, 'What are we doing with today?' . . . Have we been guilty of declaring, 'I've been thinking about making some course corrections in my life. I plan to take the first step—tomorrow'? With such thinking, tomorrow is forever. Such tomorrows rarely come unless we do something about them today."[13]

With that in mind, now might be a good time to reevaluate our goals and aspirations, rethink our direction and purpose in life, and refocus our efforts and energy on worthwhile endeavors.

The present becomes the past in a moment, so before it does, make the most of it. The future, which is really just the unfolding present, is bright for those who take the time, as the proverb counsels, to "ponder the path of [your] feet" (Proverbs 4:26).

This is the day to live, to change, to grow, and to move into the future. As Amulek testified, "This life is the time for men to prepare to meet God; yea, behold the day of this life is the day for men to perform their labors. . . . Do not procrastinate the day of your repentance until the end" (Alma 34:32–33).

Our Heavenly Father is the One who determines the number of years we have here on earth, but life is forever. Our time horizon is eternal. In our theology, we could illustrate our eternal existence with a diagram like the one below:

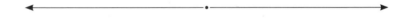

Each day well lived moves us into a better future, a better eternity.

The dot represents the years we have in mortality. The line to the left of the dot, which extends eternally, represents our premortal existence. And the line to the right, which also extends forever, represents our postmortal life.

Now, some may look at that dot and conclude that mortality is insignificant compared to eternity. That is a valid conclusion and one that can help us put some of our mortal difficulties in their proper perspective. We definitely should not expend all of our energy living for the dot when the line of eternity lies before us.

But we also should not minimize the importance of the dot.

The trajectory of the rest of the line depends on it! It is a pivotal point in our eternal existence.

What happens when we pass the dot? Are second chances over? When someone passes from this life to the next with unresolved issues and the need for another chance, will they have opportunity to change?

As Latter-day Saints, we have a unique perspective on questions like these. While we know that "this day of life . . . is given us to prepare for eternity" (Alma 34:33), we also know that the gospel is preached to the dead, and they are given the opportunity to repent. "It may not all be accomplished in this life," President Boyd K. Packer taught. "We know from visions and visitations that the servants of the Lord continue the work of redemption beyond the veil."[14] This is another way in which the gospel of Jesus Christ sets right things that have gone afoul. The Atonement of Jesus Christ fully compensates for *all* unfair disadvantages suffered during mortality, including never having the opportunity of hearing the fulness of the gospel, or never fully learning or understanding it, having been "blinded by the craftiness of men" (D&C 76:75).

One family described the peace they felt in the midst of their heartache when a rebellious teenager passed prematurely from this life into the next. Instead of despairing, as many thought they might, they found comfort in quiet moments. They knew that their precious daughter, no matter how errant, was loved by her Heavenly Father and that His plan for her happiness did not end with her death. In fact, they felt a renewed hope that somehow she might be able to see things more clearly and be able to change. It might take longer, it might be harder, but they felt that her process of learning and growth and change did not end with her death. Several years later, they felt that their hopes were confirmed when they performed temple work in her behalf. They experienced an outpouring of the Spirit, a witness to their hearts that not only was she prepared to receive those saving ordinances but that she had accepted them.

In a 1929 general conference address, Elder Orson F. Whitney, a member of the Quorum of the Twelve Apostles, repeated these teachings of the Prophet Joseph Smith: "Though some of the sheep may wander, the eye of the Shepherd is upon them, and sooner or later they will feel the tentacles of Divine Providence reaching out after them and drawing them back to the fold. *Either in this life or the life to come,* they will return. They will have to pay their debt to justice; they will suffer for their sins; and may tread a thorny path; but if it leads them at last, like the penitent Prodigal, to a loving and forgiving father's heart and home, the painful experience will not have been in vain. Pray for your careless and disobedient children; hold on to them with your faith. Hope on, trust on, till you see the salvation of God."[15]

Clearly, it is not our privilege to judge whether another person deserves a second chance—in this life or the next, today or next week. It is our privilege to hope, pray, and believe in the gospel of second chances.

CHAPTER 6

ACKNOWLEDGING THE POSSIBILITY OF CHANGE

Our heavenly Father is more liberal in His views,
and boundless in His mercies and blessings,
than we are ready to believe or receive.

JOSEPH SMITH

Although many in the world never receive a second chance because they think they don't need one, some faithful people suffer from the opposite problem—it's not that they don't think they need to change; rather, they think they can't. Perhaps they feel their mistakes are just too great; perhaps they doubt God's ability to save them; perhaps they doubt His willingness to do so. Or maybe they simply subscribe to the pessimism expressed by novelist F. Scott Fitzgerald, who wrote, "There are no second acts in American lives."[1]

As we've already seen, the overwhelming number of scriptural examples is evidence that God wants us to believe in second chances. In addition, He inspires His modern-day prophets and apostles to testify that no one is beyond the reach of the saving and renewing power of the Atonement. Following are just a few examples.

In speaking about what he calls the brilliant morning of forgiveness, President Boyd K. Packer taught:

"Save for the exception of the very few who defect to perdition, there is no habit, no addiction, no rebellion, no transgression, no apostasy, no crime exempted from the promise of complete forgiveness. That is the promise of the Atonement of Christ.

"How all can be repaired, we do not know. . . . That great morning of forgiveness may not come at once. Do not give up if at first you fail. Often the most difficult part of repentance is to forgive yourself. Discouragement is part of that test. Do not give up. That brilliant morning will come."[2]

President Thomas S. Monson encourages us with these words: "The passage of time has not altered the capacity of the Redeemer to change men's lives. As He said to the dead Lazarus, so He says to you and to me, 'Come forth' (John 11:43). I add: Come forth from the despair of doubt. Come forth from the sorrow of sin. Come forth from the death of disbelief. Come forth to a newness of life."[3]

In an article prepared in the months before he passed away, President James E. Faust wrote: "Each one of us has been given the power to change his or her life. As part of the Lord's great plan of happiness, we have individual agency to make decisions. We can decide to do better and to be better. . . .

"Each new day that dawns can be a new day for us to begin to change. We can change our environment. We can change our lives by substituting new habits for old. We can mold our character and future by purer thoughts and nobler actions. As someone once put it, 'The possibility of change is always there, with its hidden promise of peace, happiness, and a better way of life.'"[4]

More recently, Elder Jeffrey R. Holland shed new light on Jesus's parable of the laborers in the vineyard by focusing on the second chance offered to the workers who were passed over until the last hour of the day:

"This is a story about God's goodness, His patience and forgiveness, and the Atonement of the Lord Jesus Christ. It is a story about generosity and compassion. It is a story about grace. It underscores the thought I heard many years ago that surely the thing God enjoys most about being God is the thrill of being merciful, especially to those who don't expect it and often feel they don't deserve it.

" . . . However late you think you are, however many chances you think you have missed, however many mistakes you feel you have made or talents you think you don't have, or however far from home and family and God you feel you have traveled, I testify that you have *not* traveled beyond the reach of divine love. It is not possible for you to sink lower than the infinite light of Christ's Atonement shines.

" . . . There is nothing . . . that you have done that cannot be undone. There is no problem which you cannot overcome. There is no dream that in the unfolding of time and eternity cannot yet be realized. Even if you feel you are the lost and last laborer of the eleventh hour, the Lord of the vineyard still stands beckoning. 'Come boldly [to] the throne of grace,' [Hebrews 4:16] and fall at the feet of the Holy One of Israel. Come and feast 'without money and without price' [Isaiah 55:1] at the table of the Lord."[5]

Indeed, regardless of the lateness of the hour or the failings and disappointments and distresses suffered throughout the day, the Lord can turn our pain into purpose, our heartache into healing. He can restore our shattered lives and souls.

Just knowing that we can be clean again is invigorating. Like a fresh blanket of snow that changes the landscape into unmarked territory, calling out to little explorers with their sleds and snow boots, the prospect of a fresh start at life can give us a sense of opportunity, possibility, and resolution. We try a little harder, reach a little farther, and somehow do a little more. What may have seemed out of reach just days before suddenly enters the realm of possibility when we resolve with a newness of heart. We all have our share of trials and tribulations, just as we have our share of joy and happiness. During the trying times, it's easy to forget the joyful times. Life can certainly be hard, but it can also be full of hope and possibility—if we just keep trying, hold onto faith in the Lord, look for the good, and accentuate the positive. Look around you with a willing heart and open mind. You'll find that although there are discouraging days and occasional setbacks, given time and patience and perseverance, things tend to work out. The great inventor Thomas Edison, who was no stranger to failure and difficulty, said, "When you have exhausted all possibilities, remember this. You haven't."[6]

Most of us don't see the learning and growth that is taking place when we're in the midst of a "growing experience." It's only later, when we look back, that we see our increased depth and development that likely could have come no other way. Remember that no matter how deep the flaw, we can recover from our past and begin again. When our sins are remitted by the atoning blood of Christ, they are truly buried in the "depths of the sea" (Micah 7:19), put out of memory (see Hebrews 8:12), and separated from us "as far as the east is from the west" (Psalm 103:12). With the precious gift of hope and forgiveness comes "the peace of God, which passeth all understanding" (Philippians 4:7).

BREAKING THE CYCLE OF FAMILY DYSFUNCTION

Of course, Satan does not want you to believe in second chances. If, however, you choose to believe in the gospel of second chances generally, he will content himself with persuading you to doubt its specific application to you. One of the many ways he does this is by spreading the idea that if you were raised in a less-than-perfect home, you are doomed to repeat that cycle in your own family. In typical satanic fashion, he takes an element of truth—the undeniable fact that the choices parents make have long-term influence on their children—and distorts and perverts it just enough to accomplish his purposes. The adversary wants us to let our past define our future. If he can convince us that we are victims of our upbringing, then he succeeds, at least partially, in robbing us of the gift he has sought to take from us since the beginning—our agency.

In the process, Satan attempts to perpetuate the cycle of family dysfunction by popularizing it. Because of his influence, fractured families are not only common but almost fashionable in some segments of society right now. Traditional, intact families, on the other hand, are dismissed as quaint, unrealistic, or even narrow-minded. "So stop aspiring for an ideal family" is the diabolical message. "It doesn't fit into modern life, and it's not possible or worth the effort. Besides, your family never has fit that mold."

But the fact is that cycles of dysfunction can be broken. They simply don't fit Heavenly Father's plan for His children, regardless of what the world is doing.

One of my students held on to the hope that the cycle of dysfunction in families really can be broken, and he wrote about his experience for a class assignment. I share a portion of it here with his permission.

This student said he came from a family filled with anger and hostility, and even though he was determined not to pass on negative patterns to the next generation, he realized shortly after he married that those patterns were resurfacing. His marriage began to suffer; everything seemed bleak and hopeless. He knew he needed to change, but he was not sure if he could. He wrote that just receiving the assurance that he could have another chance, that he could change, that he could create a different family pattern, gave him the strength to begin the process:

"As I sat one day in the temple, the Spirit touched me. My heart had been heavy for many days, but now, for the first time in months, I felt hope. I decided that I would change and not pass on those negative patterns in my new family. I knew I needed to take responsibility and change. I had spent far too much time blaming my wife, my parents, and so many others for all my problems. It's now been a few years, but I can honestly say that I'm different today from what I was before. I've *really* changed. It hasn't been easy, and it didn't happen overnight. The Lord helped me; my wife helped me; a good bishop and good friends helped me; going to the temple, praying, and reading my scriptures helped me. Our marriage is now better than ever. I know we still have a long way to go, but now after eight years of marriage, we've never been better. I feel so grateful that I chose to listen to that prompting from the Lord and change."

"This Is Who I Am"

In the process of changing, this student discovered who he really is. He realized that he had an eternal spiritual parentage that defined him more than his earthly upbringing or his own mistakes.

It's an easy trap to fall into. How many times have we heard ourselves say, with stifling finality, "That's just the way I am"? It's usually closely followed by phrases like "I'm not a morning person," or "I'm not a people person," or "I've never been good at math," or worse, "I'm not the spiritual type."

This is what Elder Neal A. Maxwell called "the devil's dissonance": Satan's attempt to have us define ourselves by our weaknesses or missteps rather than by our divine potential.[7]

We are, before all else, children loved by God, in whose image we are created, and in whose love we are grounded, changed, and empowered. We can know with confidence that we worship a God whose love is constant and perfect, whose mercy is continuous and flawless.

"You are His child all the time," declared President Gordon B. Hinckley, "not just when you are good. You are His child when you are bad. You have within you . . . a portion of divinity that is real and tremendous and marvelous and wonderful."[8]

And what about those times when we aren't quite living up to the divinity within us? That's when the Atonement can give us a second chance to discover our true and best selves through spiritual rebirth. This is what makes the clever lie "That's just who I am" so damaging; it denies not only our divine identity but also the Savior's redeeming power.

In reality, to be born again is to truly know our very essence, stripped of all the layered accoutrements that attach to us over time and, in knowing, to become a "new creature" (2 Corinthians 5:17). To be spiritually reborn is to experience the regeneration of our nature and our character, to become changed in Christ. This relationship to Christ embodies not just a new identity but actually our true identity—*who* and *whose* we really are. Understanding that is an important step to developing the faith we need to change. The "mighty change" transforms our identity and our nature (Alma 5:14). God's gift of a second chance truly is an opportunity to start over, to live anew, to be "born again." It doesn't matter how old we are or how many failed attempts we experience before we finally become "new creatures" (Mosiah 27:25–26).

C. S. Lewis describes the "new men" in this way: "Every now and then one meets them. Their very voices and faces are different from ours: stronger, quieter, happier, more radiant. They begin where most of us leave off. They are, I say, recognisable; but you must know what to look for. . . . They do not draw attention to themselves. . . . They love you more than other men do, but they need you less."[9]

If you read a description like that and think, "That's not me," be careful! That's Satan's trap and Satan's lie. Even if it doesn't sound like you right now, that's the real you! That's what your Father is like, and you've inherited His attributes. They just need to be developed.

Is there a more powerful truth than this? "What could inspire one to purity and worthiness more," asked President Boyd K. Packer, "than to possess a spiritual confirmation that we are the children of God? What could inspire a more lofty regard for oneself, or engender more love for mankind?"[10] That assurance, noted Elder Dallin H. Oaks, can act as a "potent antidepressant that can strengthen each of us to make righteous choices and to seek the best that is within us. . . . [It can give us the] self-respect and motivation to move against the problems of life."[11] And President Thomas S. Monson taught that knowing we are children of God allows us "to face trouble with courage, disappointment with cheerfulness, and triumph with humility. . . . We cannot sincerely hold this conviction without experiencing a profound new sense of strength and power, even the strength to live the commandments of God [and] to resist the temptations of Satan."[12]

Because He is our true and loving Father, God will stand with us in times of trouble and danger. He will not leave us to face our challenges alone. He often refers to us as His "little children" (for example, John 13:33), and He will patiently work with us as we falteringly try to emulate Him, just as we do with our own children. As Elder Neal A. Maxwell lovingly reminded us: "Our perfect Father does not expect us to be perfect children yet. He had only one such Child. Meanwhile, therefore, sometimes with smudges on our cheeks, dirt on our hands, and shoes untied, stammeringly but smilingly we present God with a dandelion— as if it were an orchid or a rose! If for now the dandelion is the best we have to offer, He receives it, knowing what we may later place on the altar. It is good to remember how young we are spiritually."[13]

Your Book Isn't Finished Yet

A woman who had made some serious mistakes confided to a friend, "I think my life had a good beginning, and it's had some good parts and hard parts. But now I wonder how it will all turn out in the end." Her friend offered this insight: "A life story isn't told in one chapter. And a book isn't finished until the last page. If you can learn from the mistakes of the past and do a little better, then you can write the next chapter better than the last. Today is the day to live, to change, to grow."

Life *is* a work in progress. There may be paragraphs or pages or whole chapters that we'd like to revise. But we cannot edit the past. And perhaps we shouldn't want to. A book with no tragedies or conflicts or challenges is a dull book, and there can always be a happy ending. President Dieter F. Uchtdorf wisely observed that the hero or heroine of every story you can think of has one thing in common: "They must overcome adversity . . . between their 'once upon a time' and 'happily ever after.'"[14] This is equally true for our life stories.

The thing to remember is that life is not like reading a book that has already been written, the ending of the story already determined. We are the writer—not the reader. We get to determine the ending. "How you react to adversity and temptation," President Uchtdorf noted, "is a critical factor in whether or not you arrive at your own 'happily ever after.'"[15]

Thankfully, we don't have to write our story alone. There is One who knows our life story from the beginning to the end. He knows where we've already been, and He knows where we need to go and where we have the potential to go. He knows our heart and desires, our strengths and weaknesses, our joys and aspirations, and our heartaches and sorrows. He is our Heavenly Father, the great Author of life. If we will let Him, He will guide us to the happy ending for which all of us hope. And if something needs to be rewritten to bring our story to that happy ending, the great Author can prepare an improved and enhanced edition. We cannot edit the past, but He can.[16]

Benjamin Franklin offered this insight when he wrote his own epitaph: "[Here lies] the body of Benjamin Franklin, . . . (like the cover of an old book, its contents torn out and stripped of its lettering and guilding) . . . ; but the work shall not be lost, for it will . . . appear once more in a new and more elegant edition, revised and corrected by the Author."[17] The great Author of life is also the Editor and Rebuilder and Healer of our life. He believes in our capacity to change, and He will help us to rejoice and be glad for this day of change.

American essayist Ralph Waldo Emerson said it this way: "Finish each day and be done with it. You have done what you could. Some blunders and absurdities no doubt crept in, forget them as soon as you can. Tomorrow is a new day; you shall begin it well and serenely."[18] Today is the day to move forward with our life.

In *The Last Battle,* the final installment of the Chronicles of Narnia series, C. S. Lewis tenderly illustrates just how much of our book still remains to be written. In the story, the children are involved in a train wreck that dispatches them to the magical world of Narnia, which is a depiction of heaven. When their adventure is drawing to a close, they express fear that they will be once again sent back to earth. But the great lion, Aslan, a symbol of Jesus Christ, shares with them the wonderful news:

"Aslan turned to them and said: 'You do not yet look so happy as I mean you to be.'

"Lucy said, 'We're so afraid of being sent away, Aslan. And you have sent us back into our own world so often.'

"'No fear of that,' said Aslan. 'Have you not guessed?'

"Their hearts leaped and a wild hope rose within them.

"'There *was* a real railway accident,' said Aslan softly. 'Your father and mother and all of you are—as you used to call it in the Shadowlands—dead. The term is over: the holiday had begun. The dream is ended: this is the morning.'

"And as He spoke He no longer looked to them like a lion; but the things that began to happen after that were so great and beautiful that I cannot write them. And for us this is the end of all the stories, and we can most truly say that they all lived happily ever after. But for them it was only the beginning of the real story. All their life in this world and all their adventures in Narnia had only been the cover and the title page: now at last they were beginning Chapter One of the Great Story which no one on earth has read: which goes on forever: in which every chapter is better than the one before."[19]

For each of us, the best part of the story lies ahead. To get there, we begin every day with a clean, blank page. No matter what's in the previous pages and chapters, the next page, the next chapter is always ours to write. As we submit our will to the true Author and trust Him, we'll find every chapter, and the finished story, to be even better than we imagined.

TRUST THE EMPOWERING LOVE OF GOD

Former British prime minister Tony Blair remembered very clearly the day his faith became personal. When he was ten years old, his father (who was an avowed atheist) suffered a severe stroke and was rushed to the hospital. Uncertain if his father would live, Tony went to school fearful of the future. His teacher, noticing the young student's anxiety, suggested that they kneel and pray for his father's recovery. Tony hesitantly whispered, "I'm afraid my father doesn't believe in God."

The teacher's reply made a lasting impression: "That doesn't matter. God believes in him. He loves him without demanding or needing love in return."[20]

Sometimes I wonder if we overcomplicate God's love for us. Perhaps we doubt that God can continue to love us when we have stumbled and made mistakes. We wonder why He would listen to us now, after we've gone so long without listening to Him. We question if it is truly possible that God knows us individually. We would do well to follow the example of Nephi, who said, "I know that he loveth his children; nevertheless, I do not know the meaning of all things" (1 Nephi 11:17). It is enough to know—and trust—that God our Father loves us.

The love of God is sometimes difficult to comprehend because it is so much higher than the imperfect, earthly version (see Isaiah 55:8–9). Our Father loves us with a perfect, constant, and encompassing love. But that doesn't mean we can always feel His love regardless of how we choose to live our lives. To feel this love, we must strive to stay close to our Father in Heaven, to build a relationship with Him, and to hold onto and remember His love during seasons of trial and temptation. As we do, we develop an intimate knowledge of the ways of the Spirit. I find that the more familiar I am with the Lord and His ways and the more I sincerely strive to become even as He is, the more likely I am to sense His absence when I move in directions without Him. Having tasted of God's love, I am motivated and inspired to repent right away so that I can experience that love once again. In this way, God's love helps me stay on track or gets me back on track when I veer off course. Truly, what we love will transform us.

Delivering a commencement address to college students, Elder Jeffrey R. Holland acknowledged that as the graduates go forward with their lives, they will likely suffer discouragement, disappointment, and even despair. "You may even make a mistake or two," he said, "and worry that the chance to succeed or be safe or be happy in life has eluded you forever because of those mistakes. But, such troubled times always pass—or at least they can if you want them to." Elder Holland quoted from a sermon of the poet and preacher John Donne: " 'But God had made no decrees to distinguish the seasons of his mercies. In paradise, the fruits were ripe the first minute, and in Heaven it is always autumn. His mercies are ever in their maturity.' " Elder Holland concluded by saying: "Above all else you have learned here, may you leave this great school secure in the promise of God's unfailing love for you. . . . If you desire God's mercy, I promise you that help will come to you."[21]

The transforming power of love is beautifully expressed in George Eliot's novel *Silas Marner*—one of many stories of second chances in the world's classic literature.[22] In this story, Silas Marner is the victim of a false accusation and a friend's betrayal. As a result, Silas becomes a recluse and miser, his heart "a locked casket." His only concern is himself, his work, and his hoard of money. When his precious gold is stolen, the loss drives Silas into a deeper gloom.

Then along comes a little girl, an orphan he names Eppie, who presents Silas with a chance at redemption, another life, a new hope for happiness. When Silas's thoughts turn to little Eppie's care and keeping, when his heart opens to her, he finds love and release from his bitterness and depression. Silas may have lost his gold, but he finds true joy in a golden-haired girl who gives him a reason for living, a second chance at life.

Like the pure love of this little child, Christ's love for us is a powerful catalyst for change. His love found its fullest and deepest expression when He took upon Himself our sins, our sorrows, our heartaches, and our afflictions. When He suffered in Gethsemane and allowed Himself to be lifted up on the cross so the demands of justice could be satisfied, His great mercy extended in our behalf (see Mosiah 15:9). Charity, the pure love of Christ, is the Atonement. In Moroni's words, "Thou hast loved the world, even unto the laying down of thy life for the world, that thou mightest take it again to prepare a place for the children of men. And now I know that this love which thou hast had for the children of men is charity; wherefore, except men shall have charity they cannot inherit that place which thou hast prepared in the mansions of thy Father" (Ether 12:33–34).

Nothing inspires us to change as profoundly as our understanding of Christ's love, as expressed through His Atonement. The more deeply we understand it—and *feel* it—the more deeply we want to change, and the more resolutely we believe we *can* change. The Atonement of Christ cleanses us of sin, which is part of the Lord's redeeming grace. But another part of the Atonement, too often overlooked, is empowerment. Grace is strength and power. Through the love and strength of Christ we can do all things (see Philippians 4:13). We need that strength every moment of every day, not just to be forgiven and to overcome sins but to resist temptation and to endure. As we trust the Lord and hold onto His outstretched hand, we are infused with power and hope and sweet assurance. We can be forgiven, we can change, and we can progress as we press forward by holding on to Christ, whose mercy is the source and substance of hope.

CHAPTER 7

ACKNOWLEDGING OUR DEPENDENCE ON THE SAVIOR

O Lord, I have trusted in thee, and I will trust in thee forever.
I will not put my trust in the arm of flesh; for I know that cursed
is he that putteth his trust in the arm of flesh. Yea, cursed is
he that putteth his trust in man or maketh flesh his arm.

2 NEPHI 4:34

In addition to acknowledging the need to change and acknowledging the possibility of change, I believe there is a third key to accepting second chances in our lives: acknowledging that we need the Savior in order to change. There are those who recognize their faults and believe they can be overcome, but they think they can do it on their own.

Admittedly, it is possible for a person to engage in self-improvement while at the same time neglecting or even outright denying the role of the Savior. But that's not the kind of change we're talking about here. We're dealing with a mighty change of heart, in which our very disposition to do evil is eliminated and our lives are cleansed from our former sins—a change in our nature so fundamental that "rebirth" is really the best way to describe it (see Mosiah 5:2). This goes much deeper and lasts longer than anything you might find in a self-help book. That's why self-help alone will never be sufficient to accomplish it. True change is not a mere product of self-discipline or robust willpower. We need the cleansing and strengthening power of Christ's Atonement. If we place our trust in anything other than the Savior, we will fall short.

THE RICH YOUNG MAN

You are familiar with the biblical story of the rich young man. He had kept the commandments all his life, but he felt in his heart that he was coming up short, that he needed to do something further, deeper, greater. His uneasiness drove him to seek Jesus and sincerely ask, on bended knee, what he needed to do to inherit eternal life.

The Savior reminded him of the commandments, and the young man affirmed that he had kept them from his youth. It is clear that the wealthy man was not trying to justify or excuse himself, because his next words were "What lack I yet?" The Savior, filled with infinite love for this young man, discerned immediately what he lacked and gave him specific instruction to sell his possessions, give the money to the poor, and become one of His disciples.

But the young man "cast . . . away . . . [his] confidence" (Hebrews 10:35). Despite striving all his life to keep the commandments, he could not keep this one, and he went away sorrowing—not indignant or rebellious but sorrowing, "for he had great possessions" (Matthew 19:22).

The Apostles were stunned. If this young man, who had kept

the commandments all his life, will find it difficult to enter the kingdom of heaven, then who can, they wondered. Jesus's answer teaches a critical lesson: Even a good man cannot be saved if he feels more dependent upon his riches than upon God.[1] Indeed, realizing our dependence upon God and our overarching need for a Savior is at the heart of second chances.

Can we see ourselves in the rich young man? As we try to keep the commandments, do we ever have a nagging worry that we are still not quite good enough, a gnawing sense that we are continually coming up short? Maybe we are disheartened and feel that we just can't do it, that the road is too long and hard, and we walk away sorrowful. Despite the other good things we may have done, when we come face to face with our foibles and weaknesses, we sometimes get discouraged and are tempted to give up or "go away sorrowing." For this man it was riches; for us it could be pride or resentment or fear or apathy or an addiction or a doubt or a dozen other things. The mistake the young man made was that in his sorrow he walked away from the One who could help him overcome his weakness, the One who could give him the second chance he needed.

There are times when our lack of confidence in the promises of the Lord and lack of trust in His redeeming love keep us from going forward, staying with it, and trying again. At times, the prospect of overcoming our weaknesses may seem about as likely as a camel squeezing through the eye of a needle, but that's the miracle of the gospel of Jesus Christ. When we fail to take a second chance—for any reason—the underlying reason is a lack of understanding of the Redeemer's Atonement.

THE KING OF THE LAMANITES

Contrast the rich young man with King Lamoni's father, king over all the Lamanites, in the Book of Mormon. Both had high social status, but other than that their backgrounds were quite different—the Lamanite king not only hadn't been keeping the commandments, he likely didn't even know what they were. But after Aaron, the missionary son of King Mosiah, taught him the gospel, the king essentially asked the same question as the rich young man: "What shall I do that I may have this eternal life of which thou hast spoken?" (Alma 22:15).

Unlike the rich young man, however, the king was willing to sacrifice everything: "I will give up all that I possess, yea, I will forsake my kingdom, that I may receive this great joy" (Alma 22:15). Aaron assured him that if he would bow down before God and repent of his sins, calling upon the name of Jesus Christ for forgiveness, he would inherit eternal life. And the king immediately prostrated himself upon the earth in prayer and received the second chance he was seeking. Shortly thereafter, the king established religious freedom in the land so that anyone could receive the gospel and feel the joy that he had felt. As a result, thousands of Lamanites joined the fold of God.

It could have been difficult for such a powerful king to acknowledge dependence on a power higher than his own. It's reasonable to assume that he was used to getting what he wanted by virtue of his own wealth or power or position. But he had come to recognize that his earthly power was nothing compared to the exalting power of Christ's Atonement.

It's something that we all need to come to realize eventually. Becoming Christlike is a continuing pursuit that we cannot accomplish on our own. *We cannot do it alone.* Our hope for salvation is in Jesus Christ alone—His perfect love and compassion, His redeeming blood and righteousness. Although we cannot fully comprehend the Atonement, each of us can partake of its enabling power and transcendent blessings. Only through the Atonement can we truly be forgiven of our sins and released from the prison of despair and the bondage of hopelessness.

"Jesus will not only bridge the chasm between the ideal and the real and thus provide that final spiritual boost into eternal life, but he will also extend to us that enabling power so essential to daily living, a power that equips us to conquer weakness and begin to partake of the divine nature," wrote Brigham Young University religious education professor Robert L. Millet. "Being in a saved condition is living in the quiet assurance that God is in his heaven, that Christ is the Lord, and that the plan of redemption is real and in active operation in our personal lives. . . . This state of salvation means we are not totally free of weakness, but it means we can proceed confidently in the Savior's promise that in him we will find strength to overcome, as well as rest and peace, here and hereafter."[2]

CHAPTER 8

MAKING THE SECOND CHANCE LAST

Our greatest glory is not in never falling,
but in rising up every time we fall.

CONFUCIUS

In the Old Testament there's a story in which God metes out a punishment that at first seems rather harsh. Actually, there are a lot of stories like that in the Old Testament, but the one I'm thinking of begins when Lot, the nephew of Abraham, decides to pitch his family's tent near the wicked city of Sodom. Not *in* Sodom, just "*toward* Sodom" (Genesis 13:12; emphasis added).

Within a short time, Lot and his family are full citizens of the city, though they're doing their best to maintain their righteousness in the midst of jaw-dropping sin and depravity. (Can we relate?) Before long, the wickedness of Sodom gets out of hand, and the Lord determines to destroy the city, sending angels to warn Lot and his family to flee. With the warning, the angels give specific instruction: "Escape for thy life; look not behind thee, . . . lest thou be consumed" (Genesis 19:17). Lot's wife, however, disregards the instruction and "looked back from behind him, and she became a pillar of salt" (Genesis 19:26).

Perhaps that punishment seems a bit extreme, but it teaches an important lesson about accepting second chances. Lot's wife perished because her focus was backward rather than forward. Elder Jeffrey R. Holland explained: "It isn't just that she looked back; she looked back *longingly*. In short, her attachment to the past outweighed her confidence in the future. That, apparently, was at least part of her sin."[1] It seems she was not prepared to take the steps of faith necessary to walk into an unknown future. Rather, she found a false sense of security in looking to a familiar but, ultimately, destructive past. In other words, she did not trust the Lord's warning and accept the second chance that was given to her. As a result, she suffered the same fate as those who never left the wicked city.

The story of Lot's wife teaches us that in accepting second chances, it may not be enough just to leave Sodom—we have to leave it behind. To make our second chance last, to ensure that we do not revert back to our old ways, we must keep our spiritual eyes looking forward with faith and hope, fully willing to leave the past behind us.

THE BENT NAIL

Sometimes leaving the past behind is easier said than done. And it's not just that we might long for our former life. More often, I think, we have trouble forgiving ourselves for our past. We needlessly insist on carrying burdens that the Savior has offered to carry for us. As a result, we place artificial limits on our abilities.

Worse, we run the risk of becoming discouraged and giving up on the second chance we've been offered.

A few years ago I received a great gift in the form of an e-mail from a man named James, who expressed gratitude for a message I wrote for *Music and the Spoken Word.* We struck up a correspondence, and I soon realized that his story captures the essence of second chances. He most graciously gave me permission to retell his story here.

James grew up in southern California as an active Latter-day Saint. He participated in the programs of the Church and made many lasting memories, but he never really became personally converted. He had never made a habit of personal prayer or scripture study; his participation in the Church was more from a social interest. When he joined the army and spent a year in South Vietnam, he slid into inactivity. Over the next twenty years, James fell into the wrong crowd, acquired some bad habits, and suffered through a failed marriage. In his words, "dark spots grew on [his] soul."

One day, his grown daughter (an active member of the Church) invited James and his second wife to attend general conference. James, who by this time had not set foot in a church building in twenty years, felt self-conscious about his long hair and wayward lifestyle. At first he declined his daughter's offer, but when she called for the third time, he agreed to go with her.

On Sunday, while they were preparing to leave for conference, James and his wife tuned in to *Music and the Spoken Word.* The message that day was titled "Lost and Found," and it retold the story of the prodigal son. James felt his heart begin to soften, and by the time they arrived at the Conference Center, James and his wife were prepared to have a beautiful experience. He recounts:

"The conference session was very moving. . . . We took our seats and immediately started to cry. The Spirit was so strong, and the talks were directed to us, as if no one else was there. President Hinckley saluted the congregation with his cane, and the love I felt for this great and humble servant of the Lord was exquisite! The years of wasted and lost time came into focus all too sharply. Our hearts were broken that afternoon, and now the healing miracle could begin."

James and his wife attended church the next Sunday and were pleasantly surprised at how warm and welcoming the people were. No one seemed to mind that he was such a rough-looking character. They looked into his heart and welcomed him to the ward.

He continues:

"All who have been involved in one way or another with this kind of reactivity know that the road to repentance is not easy. There can't be any hedging or avoidance of tearful sessions with the bishop and the stake president. It was tough work, but those great leaders in [our] ward kept us focused and feeling good about ourselves. In a few weeks the long hair and beard were trimmed and cut. Not even a mustache remained. But the miracle of forgiveness is felt deeper than that. Broken hearts began to be mended, and spiritual deficits started to change into strengths. Temple plans were looked forward to with hopeful joy."

As time went by, James and his wife not only became fully

active in the Church, paid their tithing, and lived the Word of Wisdom but also entered the house of the Lord and made temple covenants. Many of their family members were able to join them on that joyous occasion.

Then, James's second chance received an unexpected trial: James was called to serve in the bishopric in his inner city ward. In his own words, he describes this personal struggle:

"Doubts and fears began to keep me up at night. I knew this was a favorite ploy that Satan enjoyed using against former sinners. I also knew that I had been forgiven of my past transgressions and that it was Jesus Christ who took my stripes and who had my name imprinted on His hands. . . . I knew the answers, but I still worried about all those wasted years filled with sin and selfishness, years that should have been growth and development years for me. Could I ever be a useful tool in the gospel plan again? At times in my human weakness, these moments of faithlessness became numbing at best and crippling at worst."

While he was struggling with these doubts, James was building a new home for his family. It was in the process of this work that James had a life-changing epiphany. At his request, his daughter had gone around the building lot with an extension magnet and gathered all of the discarded bent and rusty nails. He remembered his grandfather showing him how to carefully pound out the kinks in bent nails, so they could be used again. While straightening the bent nails, James made an interesting discovery:

"These rehabilitated nails, having some kinks and wear still on the steel shank, were better at holding fast than the brand new nails. They simply took hold of the wood better.

"As I pondered this, the Spirit gave me witness of the truth I had just found. Faith began to replace nagging fears once and for all on this matter. I was useful after all! My experiences could be applied to all kinds of gospel situations. Perhaps they could even be used to shore up another in the process of being rescued from life's pitfalls. This miracle was received into a prepared heart with gladness and thankfulness."

James has a strong testimony that we worship a God of second chances. He now keeps one of those straightened nails in his top drawer next to his tie tacks and often carries it to church in his suit pocket. He thanks the Lord that he was given another chance and has made it his life's mission to help others find their way. He concludes:

"How grateful my wife and I are for Jesus Christ, the Lord of second chances, the carpenter's son who lovingly straightens bent and misshapen nails and uses them again in this great and marvelous gospel plan. We still have our challenges and struggles today, but we know that we are pointed in the right direction. We have all we need to make it home again. Like Nephi of old, we may not yet understand the meaning of all things, but we know that God loves us. That is sufficient for the day!"

As my friend James discovered, the Savior can make use of any humble, willing soul—regardless of his or her past—if we turn to Him and trust Him. Healing and growth blossom when we put our faith and hope in the Lord and, step by step, learn to place our full trust in Him. Always remember, the Lord loves bent nails and broken hearts, sinners and Saints, and all who come to Him for rescue and redemption and rebirth. Our love and praise and thanksgiving overflow with sweet rejoicing for the Lord and His gospel of second chances.

LEAVE IT BURIED

One important lesson my friend learned was that we are not fully taking advantage of our second chance until we have fully forgiven ourselves. To paraphrase the words of the Lord to Peter, don't persist in calling unclean what God Himself has cleansed (see Acts 10:15). Have faith in the cleansing power of the Atonement, and allow yourself to believe that the Lord can make of your life something more beautiful than you can imagine.

Several years ago, Elder Shayne M. Bowen of the Seventy spoke of two beautiful landmarks in Idaho Falls, Idaho: a large regional airport and nearby Freeman Park. These useful and attractive facilities are remarkable, he explained, because both were built on top of landfills. Years and years of garbage filled up low-lying land and was covered with earth. On top of those landfills, the city of Idaho Falls built a busy airport and a peaceful, family-friendly park.

Elder Bowen noted that he had lived in Idaho Falls for most of his life and had "contributed a lot of garbage to those landfills over the course of more than 50 years. What would the city fathers think," he wondered, "if on a given day I showed up on one of the runways of the Idaho Falls airport or the middle of one of the grassy fields in Freeman Park with a backhoe and started digging large holes? When they asked me what I was doing, I would respond that I wanted to dig up the old garbage that I had made over the years.

"I suspect they would tell me that there was no way to identify my personal garbage, that it had been reclaimed and buried long ago. I'm sure that they would tell me that I had no right to dig up the garbage and that I was destroying something very beautiful and useful that they had made out of my garbage. In short, I don't think they would be very pleased with me. I suppose that they would wonder why anyone would want to destroy something so beautiful and useful in an attempt to dig up old garbage."[2]

It seems ridiculous, but how many of us do exactly that with our own past sins and mistakes? Through the miracle of His Atonement, the Savior has not only covered up our sins but has turned the whole landscape into something beautiful, useful, and so far removed from its undesirable past that it's almost unbelievable. But we must believe it. Believing in second chances means believing in miracles. It means believing that a landfill can become a beautiful park that thousands of people enjoy year after year without ever giving any thought to the fact that it used to be a landfill. It means believing that an airport is in no way less useful or less effective because there is decades-old garbage buried deep under the runway; the planes can still run on time, and passengers can still have a pleasant experience—unless someone shows up with a backhoe looking to unearth some old trash. Believing in second chances means letting the Savior bury our past—and then leaving it buried.

Making the Second Time Different

Receiving a second chance can and should change how we see ourselves. It should change our outlook on life. We should be different than we were before. Our attitude might be similar to the one Michael Robinson expressed when he wrote:

"Had I the chance to live life over, I would do things somewhat differently. I would understand at the beginning that much of our life is spent in vain pursuits. If I could do it again, I would hate less and love more, work less overtime and spend more time with my family, argue less and listen more, collect fewer debts and more friends.

"If God granted me a second chance, I would grow closer to living things—to petunias, to aspen trees, to kittens, to my children. Bedtime stories would be as important as news stories; valentines and birthdays would be as honored as paydays. I would never go to bed without saying to someone, 'I love you,' or without experiencing the beauty of a song, a poem, or a painting.

"And finally, each morning as I arose I would repeat these words: The past is gone and tomorrow may never come . . . I will live for today."[3]

Isn't this the way we should see our second chance—as an opportunity to do things differently, not as license to experiment with life for a while, keeping the Atonement in our back pocket like a "Get Out of Jail Free" card to be pulled out and played when we need it? Elder Richard L. Evans expressed the warning this way: "We all make mistakes. If our repentance is sincere, we have the right to approach [Heavenly Father] for forgiveness, but remember we are not entitled to any quota of mistakes. It is *always* better that we don't make them. And surely we shouldn't go on stupidly or stubbornly repeating the same old mistakes over and over again. We ought to have learned our lessons. It isn't enough to be just as good today as we were yesterday. We should be better."[4] When the Lord does give us a second chance, we must do everything we can to make the second time different—to *live* differently, to *become* different, because of the marvelous gift we have received.

President James E. Faust observed: "I believe firmly in the gospel of the second chance. But the gospel of the second chance means that having once been found weak, as was Peter when he denied that he knew the Savior, thereafter we become steadfast like the few Lamanites spoken of in Third Nephi, 'They were firm, and steadfast, and immovable, willing with all diligence to keep the commandments of the Lord' (3 Nephi 6:14)."[5]

Many years ago, the well-known preacher Billy Sunday said that the reason Christians fall into sin so often is because they treat temptation like strawberry shortcake rather than a rattle-snake! The best way to avoid sin is to avoid temptation. We can trust the scriptural promise: "There hath no temptation taken you but such as is common to man: but God is faithful, who will not suffer you to be tempted above that ye are able; but will with the temptation also make a way to escape, that ye may be able to bear it" (1 Corinthians 10:13). But that promise does not work if we are overly hospitable to temptation.

While Sister Julie B. Beck was serving as a member of the Young Women general presidency, she was asked what young people can do about the many temptations that surround them. She responded by sharing this analogy:

"If you're on a non-chocolate-chip-cookie diet, yet you go into the kitchen just after the cookies have been baked—it smells delicious and you can picture the chocolate chips melting as you pull the cookie apart—how long is it going to be before you sample one? How strong are you really? That's resisting—or trying to resist. But if you're on a non-chocolate-chip-cookie diet and you don't go into the kitchen where they're baked and you don't bake them yourself, then you are avoiding temptation. That's easier!"[6]

THEY "NEVER DID FALL AWAY"

Perhaps the best example of making second chances last is, not surprisingly, in the Book of Mormon, that book about second chances. There we find the story of a "wild and a hardened and a ferocious people; a people who delighted in murdering the Nephites, and robbing and plundering them; and their hearts were set upon riches, or upon gold and silver, and precious stones; yet they sought to obtain these things by murdering and plundering, that they might not labor for them with their own hands" (Alma 17:14).

But then the sons of Mosiah brought them the gospel of Jesus Christ, and they changed dramatically. Where once they were wild and ferocious and murderous, they became peaceful. Where once they delighted in killing the Nephites, they became friends and great allies with their brethren. Where once they would do anything for riches—short of working for them—they became hard workers who would do anything for the Lord. They would quite literally rather die than commit sin. In fact, their conversion was so thorough that they earned the following praise from Mormon, the compiler of the record: "I say unto you, as the Lord liveth, as many of the Lamanites as believed in their preaching, and were converted unto the Lord, never did fall away" (Alma 23:6). How many missionaries wish they could say that about the people they taught!

So how did they do it? How did they make their second chance so permanent?

There are probably many answers, but one that stands out is their decision to bury their weapons of war—the symbols of the murderous and rebellious ways of their past—deep in the earth and covenant with the Lord never again to shed blood. Here are the words of their king proposing this idea to his people:

"Now, my best beloved brethren, since God hath taken away our stains, and our swords have become bright, then let us stain our swords no more with the blood of our brethren.

"Behold, I say unto you, Nay, let us retain our swords that they be not stained with the blood of our brethren; for perhaps, if we should stain our swords again they can no more be washed bright through the blood of the Son of our great God, which shall be shed for the atonement of our sins. . . .

"Oh, how merciful is our God! And now behold, since it has been as much as we could do to get our stains taken away from us, and our swords are made bright, let us hide them away that they may be kept bright, as a testimony to our God at the last day, or at the day that we shall be brought to stand before him to be judged, that we have not stained our swords in the blood of our brethren since he imparted his word unto us and has made us clean thereby.

"And now, my brethren, if our brethren seek to destroy us,

behold, we will hide away our swords, yea, even we will bury them deep in the earth, that they may be kept bright, as a testimony that we have never used them, at the last day; and if our brethren destroy us, behold, we shall go to our God and shall be saved" (Alma 24:12–16).

It wasn't long before their brethren *did* seek to destroy them. But as their fellow Lamanites (those who had not been converted) attacked, they refused to fight back, and thousands died. This was the price they were willing to pay rather than even *approach* their former sins.

To me this seems like the personification of the Lord's promise we find later in the Book of Mormon: "If men come unto me I will show unto them their weakness. I give unto men weakness that they may be humble; and my grace is sufficient for all men that humble themselves before me; for if they humble themselves before me, and have faith in me, then will I make weak things become strong unto them" (Ether 12:27). Through the grace of Christ in the lives of these converted Lamanites, where delighting in bloodshed was their great weakness, their courageous refusal to kill—even in self-defense—became their great strength. Warmongers became peacemakers. Sinners became saints. That's the miracle of second chances.

What can we learn from their example? One clear lesson is that in order to make our second chance permanent, there may be symbolic swords and weapons of rebellion that we need to bury. There may be something in our lives that we need to eliminate—to show the Lord and ourselves that we are serious about changing. As was the case with these Lamanites, the thing we choose to bury may not be inherently evil, except that for us it represents—and may even return us to—our former sinful ways. Doing this may require sacrifice, though usually not the sacrifice of our lives; more often, it will be the sacrifice of some *part* of our lives, some worldly thing, perhaps, that is good but not essential to retaining our change of heart. Maybe there are some hobbies we need to discontinue or some associations we should avoid. What we learn from the converted Lamanites is that no such sacrifice is too great if it leads us finally to stand before the Lord free of stain, able to testify to Him that once we received our second chance, we "never did fall away."

CONVERSION IS A PROCESS, NOT AN EVENT

Not long ago in our ward, a young elder, about to leave the country for his mission, shed new light on an old principle as he spoke of one of his favorite people in the Book of Mormon: Corianton, the son of Alma who fell into sin—at least that's what most of us remember about him. The soon-to-depart elder explained that he loved Corianton not because of the mistakes he made but because of his repentance. He observed that Corianton's repentance process was much like so many of ours. He was not visited by an angel. He did not have any dramatic experiences that led to his change of heart. He simply began and then continued the difficult process of becoming clean.

The exciting—yet often overlooked—part of Corianton's story comes in this somewhat understated verse of scripture: "There was continual peace among [the Nephites], and exceedingly great prosperity in the church because of their heed and diligence which they gave unto the word of God, which was declared unto them by Helaman, and Shiblon, and Corianton, and Ammon and his brethren, yea, and by all those who had been ordained by the holy order of God" (Alma 49:30). Without fanfare, Corianton is included in a list of faithful priesthood holders whose preaching brought peace and prosperity to the Church.

The elder concluded that the story of Corianton's forgiveness is not explicitly laid out in the Book of Mormon, probably because it was not a single event like his father Alma's or Enos's or Lamoni's. But the effects that the Atonement had on Corianton, while not as dramatic as some, were just as powerful.

Like Corianton, this young elder went into the mission field with the gospel of second chances and the power of the Atonement burning in his heart. He understood something that all of us must come to understand as we seek our own second chance: Most of the people who exercise faith, repent of their sins, and keep the commandments receive a remission of their sins through a gradual process rather than a singular, remarkable event (see Helaman 3:35; Moroni 8:25–26). Little by little, line upon line, over time and across space, we eventually can change for the better. It's that slow and steady process that works in us a mighty change of heart.

In fact, it could be argued that even those who experience a dramatic conversion must also have a steady, sustained, ongoing conversion experience to maintain their change of heart long term. Consider Alma the Younger, for example. Few conversion experiences have been more dramatic than his: He went from persecutor to prophet on the strength of an angelic visitation that shook the earth and put him in a three-day-long coma. And yet when Alma bears his testimony to the people of Zarahemla, he does it in these words:

"Do ye not suppose that I know of these things myself? Behold, I testify unto you that I do know that these things whereof I have spoken are true. And how do ye suppose that I know of their surety?

"Behold, I say unto you they are made known unto me by the Holy Spirit of God. Behold, I have fasted and prayed many days that I might know these things of myself. And now I do know of myself that they are true; for the Lord God hath made them manifest unto me by his Holy Spirit; and this is the spirit of revelation which is in me" (Alma 5:45–46).

Alma didn't say, "I know these things of myself because an angel came down and spoke to me directly with a voice of thunder, and it's pretty hard to deny that." Instead, Alma tells us he gained his testimony the same way you and I do: by fasting and praying and listening to the Holy Ghost.

President Ezra Taft Benson counseled us not to become discouraged by expecting the sensational or by comparing our experiences with those of others:

"We must be careful, as we seek to become more and more godlike, that we do not become discouraged and lose hope. Becoming Christlike is a lifetime pursuit and very often involves growth and change that is slow, almost imperceptible. . . . The scriptures record remarkable accounts of men whose lives changed dramatically, in an instant, as it were: Alma the Younger, Paul on the road to Damascus, Enos praying far into the night,

King Lamoni. Such astonishing examples of the power to change even those steeped in sin give confidence that the Atonement can reach even those deepest in despair.

"But we must be cautious as we discuss these remarkable examples. Though they are real and powerful, they are the exception more than the rule. For every Paul, for every Enos, and for every King Lamoni, there are hundreds and thousands of people who find the process of repentance much more subtle, much more imperceptible. Day by day they move closer to the Lord, little realizing they are building a godlike life. They live quiet lives of goodness, service, and commitment. They are like the converted Lamanites, who the Lord said 'were baptized with fire and with the Holy Ghost, and they knew it not' (3 Nephi 9:20)."

President Benson continued: "We must not lose hope. Hope is an anchor to the souls of men. Satan would have us cast away that anchor. In this way he can bring discouragement and surrender. But we must not lose hope. The Lord is pleased with every effort, even the tiny, daily ones in which we strive to be more like Him. Though we may see that we have far to go on the road to perfection, we must not give up hope."[7]

Indeed, conversion is a lifelong process for all of us. Even Paul, Alma, and King Lamoni were not done after their transformative experience; even they had to stay with it, day after day, in righteousness. The Atonement works within each of us over time, little by little, day by day. This is why, in His loving mercy, the Lord commanded us to take the sacrament *weekly*. He knew that we would regularly need to repent of our sins and renew our covenants.

Another Christian writer said this about the phenomenon of being "born again, and again": "When people talk about conversion experiences I think less of a drop-to-your-knees, lightning-bolt moment of heavenly clarity than about a recurring choice that presents itself at every turn—however momentous or quotidian—of every day. In each instance, we choose to believe either that God is in our hearts or he is not, and the content of that choice reveals the texture of our faith. . . . In choosing faith over ease, God over Caesar, we are (at least in that moment) born again."[8]

Rebirth, then, is not so much a moment as a mindset, an ongoing experience of the heart, the gradual accumulation of countless righteous choices built up over a lifetime. It is a daily decision to sincerely accept the Lord's invitation to discipleship: "If any man will come after me, let him deny himself, and take up his cross daily, and follow me" (Luke 9:23).

The path of discipleship becomes clearer the longer we stay on it, but it is a process that takes patience. Be assured that your efforts and your desires are known to the Lord; He sees your steps of faith and obedience and perseverance—however small and imperceptible they may seem to you. He knows your heart, and you know enough of His heart to know that He loves you perfectly and continuously. As the Apostle Paul powerfully wrote to the Romans: "Who shall separate us from the love of Christ? shall tribulation, or distress, or persecution, or famine, or nakedness, or peril, or sword? . . . Nay, in all these things we are more than conquerors through him that loved us. For I am persuaded, that neither death, nor life, nor angels, nor principalities, nor powers, nor things present, nor things to come, nor height, nor depth, nor any other creature, shall be able to separate us from the love of God, which is in Christ Jesus our Lord" (Romans 8:35, 37–39).

When life hurts and heartache comes, when challenges intensify—which they will—we can hold onto hope. After we have been "sanctified by the Holy Ghost, having [our] garments made white, being pure and spotless before God, [we cannot] look upon sin save it were with abhorrence" (Alma 13:12). This is what it means to have "a mighty change" in our hearts, with "no more disposition to do evil, but to do good continually" (Mosiah 5:2)—to do more than talk the talk, but to walk the walk of discipleship. It is a result of Christ's Atonement working in our hearts.

"Is This the Movie I Remember?"

Sometimes we are changed so incrementally, so steadily over time, that we may not even realize how far we have come until we return to a former comfort zone and realize that we are no longer comfortable there. For example, many years ago, I wanted to share with my children a movie I had enjoyed while I was in college. I remembered it was filled with hilarity and high adventure, and it carried a PG rating (there was no PG-13 in those days), so I felt safe showing it to my family.

What a mistake!

I gathered the children together, put the DVD into the player, and pushed Play. We all watched with eager anticipation to see this movie of which I had spoken so highly. Within a few minutes, though, I thought, "Is this the same movie I remember?" The profanity started, then an inappropriate scene and innuendo, then more profanity and more innuendo. We watched a little more, fast-forwarded past more, watched a little more. I kept waiting for it to get better, funnier, more adventurous. It didn't.

We ejected the DVD. The kids were disappointed; I was embarrassed. My sincere apologies to our children came next, and a lesson was learned: The movie had not changed; *I had changed.* It was no longer funny, just stupid. It was certainly not high adventure, just base entertainment.

This incident was a revelation for me. I was disappointed with myself but also, upon more reflection, gratified to know that my tastes had changed over the years. What was once funny and entertaining was now degrading; what was once acceptable was now morally offensive and a waste of time. It was a good teaching moment for my children and for me. My change was so gradual that I hadn't noticed it—but the change was definitely real.

Constantly believing in, hoping for, and seeking life's second chances gives us the confidence to live a life that, while not flawless, is determined; not perfect, but steadily progressing. And it's not just second chances—sometimes third, fourth, fifth, and more chances are needed as we learn and grow along our life's course. Truly, the only time you run out of chances is when you stop taking them.

This process can be frustrating at times, especially when it seems that we are constantly struggling with the same problems over and over again, and we can't see that we're making much progress. In such situations, it helps to remember what Elder Dallin H. Oaks taught about the ultimate goal of this process. "The Final Judgment," he said, "is not just an evaluation of a sum total of good and evil acts—what we have *done.* It is an acknowledgment of the final effect of our acts and thoughts—what we have *become.* It is not enough for anyone just to go through the motions. The commandments, ordinances, and covenants of the gospel are not a list of deposits required to be made in some heavenly account. The gospel of Jesus Christ is a plan that shows us how to become what our Heavenly Father desires us to become."[9]

We are the sons and daughters of God, who desires that we become like Him and inherit all that He has, as President George Q. Cannon testified: "We are the children of God, and as His children there is no attribute we ascribe to Him that we do not possess, though they may be dormant or in embryo. The mission of the Gospel is to develop those powers and make us like our Heavenly Parent. I know this is true, and such knowledge makes me feel happy."[10] Never forget that God is there. The message is the same to everyone: hang on, stay with it, don't ever give up. Don't ever lose hope. Every second chance comes with the knowledge that we will never attain perfection in this life. But the earthly effort and struggle is worth it because it gets us that much closer. A second chance is another step in our journey of growth and development. God is more concerned with the final outcome than in our stumbles along the way.

In the scriptures, the process is often known as enduring to the end: "He that endureth to the end, the same shall be saved. And now, my beloved brethren, I know by this that unless a man shall endure to the end, in following the example of the Son of the living God, he cannot be saved" (2 Nephi 31:15–16). Every one of us is called upon to endure to the end, to remain steadfast and true—"relying wholly upon the merits of him who is mighty to save" (2 Nephi 31:19)—until we have safely passed into the world to come.[11]

Just because change happens gradually and almost imperceptibly, however, doesn't mean it happens automatically. Enduring to the end is not a passive experience. It is both patient and proactive, serene and unwearied; it means striving, working, bearing trials with fortitude, hoping and trusting in the Lord, and then acting on that hope, even when the desires of our hearts are delayed. It means actively combating Satan's weapons of fear and doubt with the fundamental virtues of discipleship: faith, hope, and charity. It means that we continue on the strait and narrow path no matter how many times we stumble or fall. It means we press forward, grasp hold of the iron rod with both hands, and keep holding on to the very end.

RAISE AN EBENEZER

Not long ago, I spoke with a young man who has struggled to overcome the effects of sin for several years. The process of repentance has been slow and arduous. He found that it was more difficult than he thought it would be to abandon his former ways and truly change. But he is doing it! Little by little, the temptations are less alluring, and he feels the strength that comes from making righteous choices. We talked about the truth that repentance is improvement and refinement motivated and empowered by Christ—and we ought to be involved every day of our lives in constantly striving to put away the folly of our fleeting world, in continually seeking divine assistance to put off the natural man and put on Christ.

He talked about a song that the Mormon Tabernacle Choir often sings that has come to have special meaning for him. "Come, Thou Fount of Every Blessing" speaks to his heart in a special way and gives him the strength to take a righteous stand and to grasp the iron rod more tightly. We talked together of a verse in the song that is perplexing to some:

> *Here I raise my Ebenezer,*
> *Hither by Thy help I'm come;*
> *And I hope, by Thy good pleasure,*
> *Safely to arrive at home.*

I asked him if he understood the line "Here I raise my Ebenezer." He told me he did not at first, but he had researched it. We talked about the prophet Samuel, who some three thousand years ago led ancient Israel to victory over a powerful enemy. Samuel placed a large stone at the place of their deliverance and dedicated it as a monument to God's assistance. He called the stone "Eben-ezer," which meant "stone of help." The stone became a symbol of the Lord's goodness and strength (1 Samuel 7:12; see also vv. 7–11.).

This practice of raising memorials to divine help has deep roots in ancient Israel. Generations earlier, after a miraculous crossing of the Jordan River, Joshua commanded the people to gather twelve stones from the river and build a monument. He explained that the purpose of the monument was to build faith in future generations, that "when [their] children ask . . . in time to come, saying, What mean ye by these stones?" they could tell their children how the Lord helped them in their hour of need (Joshua 4:6; see also vv. 1–5, 7).

The practice continued into the time of Christ and seems to have been on Peter's mind after he witnessed the glorious manifestations on the Mount of Transfiguration. "Lord, it is good for us to be here," he said. "If thou wilt, let us make here three tabernacles; one for thee, and one for Moses, and one for Elias" (Matthew 17:4). When we have a meaningful experience with the Savior's grace and power, we naturally want to hold onto it, to make this spiritual event somehow more tangible, perhaps even more permanent—if for no other reason than to go back to that moment, whenever times get tougher, and remember what we felt.

The young man and I talked about the truth that each of us could "raise an Ebenezer," a memorial or remembrance of the divine assistance, heavenly favor, and forgiveness extended to us. Just as the people of Ammon buried the physical representation of their sins, it may be helpful to hold close a physical representation of our second chance. Our Ebenezer may not be a monument of stone—indeed, hearts filled with humility and gratitude are the most meaningful memorials. Whatever form our Ebenezer takes (a painting of the Savior, a picture of the temple, a favorite hymn or scripture, a CTR ring, or a bent nail), it can remind us of our righteous resolutions and renew our hope that by the Lord's good pleasure and in His due time, we will safely arrive home. We will become all that He intends for us to become.

CHAPTER 9

GIVING OTHERS
A SECOND CHANCE

*Haven't we wished with all the energy of our souls
for mercy—to be forgiven for the mistakes we have made
and the sins we have committed? Because we all depend on the
mercy of God, how can we deny to others any measure
of the grace we so desperately desire for ourselves?*

DIETER F. UCHTDORF

Most of us are familiar with Charles Dickens's *A Christmas Carol.* In this classic tale of second chances, the ghost of Jacob Marley, weighed down by the chains of selfishness he forged in life, visits mean-spirited Ebenezer Scrooge and tries to give his former business partner a second chance. Because Marley sets in motion a series of ghostly visitations, all is not lost for Scrooge, who sees his past, present, and future and undergoes a change of heart. The message is clear: There is hope for everyone. Even a callous, selfish old man can change. The marvel is not that Scrooge began to suddenly think of others and spend money in their behalf; the marvel is that there was a change in the inner man, a mighty change of heart, a transformation of the soul.

It is a heartwarming story that resonates in our hearts, perhaps because it portrays so powerfully this timeless principle of second chances. But to me, there is a rather tragic aspect to this story that never fully gets resolved. In fact, it replays itself every year, especially around Christmastime.

When you hear the word *scrooge,* what do you think of? Merriam-Webster's dictionary defines *scrooge* as "a miserly person."[1] Not "a person who was once miserly but who, when given a second chance, chose to reform his life and share his wealth with those less fortunate." Just "a miserly person." Even though everyone knows how Scrooge's story ends, his name has nevertheless entered our consciousness (and our dictionary) as the embodiment of what he once was—not what he ultimately became. To me, that is the unresolved tragedy of Dickens's story.

The same thing has happened to the word *grinch.* We are all familiar with the character in Dr. Seuss's *How the Grinch Stole Christmas;* we all know that because of his disillusionment with the commercialization of Christmas (and who can't identify with that?), the Grinch tries to "steal" Christmas by stealing its materialistic excesses. And we also know about the change of heart he experiences when he comes to appreciate the true spirit of Christmas, after the trappings have been stripped away. And yet, if we meet someone who has come to appreciate the real meaning of Christmas as the Grinch did, would we say, "He's a real grinch"? No! *Grinch* is defined in our English as a "killjoy, spoilsport."[2] The poor Grinch is immortalized for his abandoned past, not his reformed future.

Perhaps the way we remember fictional characters in Christmas stories is of little consequence; however, the way we think of our friends, neighbors, and family members is paramount. Do we sometimes define people in terms of who they have been rather than who they are or who they can become? As we seek second chances for ourselves, do we subtly, perhaps subconsciously, deny second chances for others?

CHANGED FOR THE BETTER

I remember well my thirty-five-year high school reunion, where I reconnected for an evening with many long-lost friends and acquaintances. At first, it was easy to see my classmates the way they were more than three decades ago, to remember the cliques and social strata and even some of the trauma of high school. But I soon discovered that life had improved nearly every one of them.

Some who had been vain and brash decades ago were now gracious and composed. Some who had been shy and retiring in high school were now more confident. Some who were wayward and rebellious were now devout and humble. One who had struggled as a senior in high school was now actively serving the Church and his community. Another who seemed destined for greatness now reflected on life's ups and downs, including the heartache of divorce, and yet he came to the reunion with a smile and opened his heart to others. Some struggled with their faith and family, and many of us had gained weight and lost hair. But while a few still clung to vestiges of adolescent vanity, most came together on cordial common ground. Age and experience had softened and enlarged almost everyone's heart. I felt that thirty-five years of joy and heartache, success and failure, growth and development had taught us a bit more to appreciate others—and ourselves—in new ways.

I realize that it was only one evening, and one can never get a complete picture from passing interactions. But this reunion was notably different from our 5- and 10- and 20-year reunions, when many of us more tenaciously held on to our pride, restricted social groupings, raging competitiveness, and acquisitiveness. In fact, I suspect that had I been able to attend each reunion over the past thirty-five years, I would have noticed an incremental softening, changing, and improving for most everyone.

Over a lifetime, most people change for the better. How often do we hear of a stubborn or irresponsible teenager who is now a family man with teenagers of his own? We've all known rowdy, restless youngsters who grew up to be competent, contributing members of their community. Maybe we think of our own immature past and feel grateful when others value us for who we *are,* rather than remembering who we *were.* And all of us appreciate it when others forgive our trespasses, overlook our mistakes, and pardon our shortcomings.

It is intriguing and disheartening to me to see how we sometimes hold on to the past so stubbornly and refuse to let others change and grow. Why do we do that? Does it somehow make us feel superior? Do the judicial robes we presume to wear help us feel better about our own lives by comparison? Perhaps it is just a very human tendency to remember people as we once knew them.

But it's wrong.

I think of modern prophets, apostles, and other priesthood

and auxiliary leaders—all of whom were once young. Do we let them grow and change? I think of the believers at the time of Alma the Younger or Zeezrom or Paul or Peter, and so many others. Were they truly able to accept the fact that these individuals had changed? I think of loved ones and friends who may have hurt us in the past. Do we let them change? I think of so many others all around us who, like us, are trying to do their best, trying to improve and become better. Do we give them a second chance?

As Jesus instituted the sacrament among the Nephites, He also taught His chosen disciples that they should not cast out the unworthy or the unrepentant who desire to partake of the sacrament. With encompassing love and an eternal perspective, the Lord exhorted His disciples to pray for those people and continue to minister to them, "*for ye know not* but what they will return and repent, and come unto me with full purpose of heart, and I shall heal them" (3 Nephi 18:32; emphasis added).

"*Let people repent,*" Elder Jeffrey R. Holland urged. "*Let people grow. Believe that people can change and improve. . . .* If something is buried in the past, leave it buried. Don't keep going back with your little sand pail and beach shovel to dig it up, wave it around, and then throw it at someone, saying, 'Hey! Do you remember *this?*' Splat!

"Well, guess what?" he continued. "That is probably going to result in some ugly morsel being dug up out of *your* landfill with the reply, 'Yeah, I remember it. Do *you* remember *this?*' Splat.

"And soon enough everyone comes out of that exchange dirty and muddy and unhappy and hurt, when what our Father in

Heaven pleads for is cleanliness and kindness and happiness and healing."[3]

While in the process of writing this book, I went to the temple one day. As I walked into the chapel, a man came up to me and wanted to shake my hand. He said, "You don't recognize me, do you?" I glanced at his name badge, and memories started to form. He reminded me that he "was a rebel in high school." I began to remember him. I went to junior high and high school with him; we knew each other quite well. I had not seen him since high school graduation decades earlier. With some chagrin, he acknowledged that he had been "wild and wayward" during those adolescent years. But now, here he was, nearly forty years later, an ordinance worker in the temple. He had a spiritual glow and warm happiness about him that inspired me and touched my heart. I thought, once more, how grateful I am for the gospel of second chances.

"LIFE TO YOU"

In Tahiti, people greet each other with the phrase *ia ora na,* which means "life to you" or "that you might live." I don't know if Tahitians think much about that phrase when they say it (any more than English speakers realize that the meaning of *good-bye* is "God be with you"), but the idea of greeting a person by "giving life" is a powerful one. Brother Russell T. Osguthorpe, general president of the Sunday School, served a mission in Tahiti, and he says that this greeting is a constant reminder to him that "we are either giving life or taking life from each other as we move forward on our way. Harsh words take life away from the one who receives them and even from the one who utters them. But words spoken in love give life."[4] I think we could extend these sentiments to include not just words but also thoughts and actions that we have toward each other. Are we giving life—or taking it away—by the things we think, say, and do?

Sometimes we need to update and reframe our thoughts of others, for our own sake and for the good of those around us. Indeed, our thoughts can be either jailors of negativity, imprisoning us in disapproval and criticism, or angels of freedom, liberating us to see potential and growth. The truth is that no one knows the full story on anybody. We're all a work in progress. If we see people only for what they appear to be now and not what they could become, then we haven't yet caught the spirit of the healing and strengthening power of the Atonement—we haven't fully understood the gospel of second chances. As a wise father recently said to me concerning his wayward son, "It's a long walk on a long road." And as a wayward son said to his mother, "Mom, please don't be too upset with me. The Lord's not finished with me yet."

Remember, failure, like success, is never final. And failure is an event, never a person. We all have successes in our past, just as we can all remember things we wish we had done a little better. Indeed, we all change—and we all can *continue* to change. As we strive to improve our own lives, may we patiently allow those around us to do the same. May our lives and relationships be enriched as we choose to embrace life's lessons that can help us change for the better. Perhaps the greatest gift we can offer each other is a second chance.

Forgiveness and the Atonement

A few years ago, the discussion in our ward high priest group meeting took an unexpected turn as we began to talk about how to deal with people who are difficult. One member of the group said, "I just try to stay out of their way; avoid them as much as possible." Another said, "Sometimes the more you get to know people the more you realize that they are not trustworthy, and you guard yourself for protection so you don't get hurt." Still another, with a little twinkle in his eye, said that he gives back as good as he gets and has learned not to back down or "play the wimp." The discussion went on for several more minutes, and then a wise and good man, our former bishop, said without a hint of self-righteousness, "I have found that the older I get and the more I get to know people, the more forgiving I am of weaknesses and imperfections. The closer I get to people and the more I get to know them, the more I like them."

We can choose to give others the benefit of the doubt. We can give second, third, fourth, and more chances and choose to love and forgive—or we can withhold forgiveness. We can "wrestle with pigs" and get dirty along with them, or we can choose the Savior's more excellent way and extend kindness and forbearance. That's not to say we shouldn't be prudent and discerning, even wise and cautious about relationships that could be harmful or destructive. Nor should we be weak victims to the whims of another. But, in tune with the Spirit, disciples of the Lord strive to err on the side of patience, compassion, and forgiveness. Followers of the Lord strive to follow His injunction to be "wise as serpents, and harmless as doves" (Matthew 10:16).

John Taylor, third President of the Church, said: "When you get the spirit of God, you feel full of kindness, charity and longsuffering, and you are willing all the day long to accord to every man that which you want yourself. You feel disposed all the day long to do unto all men as you would wish them to do unto you."[5] It is the Spirit that opens our hearts to forgiveness, mercy, and compassion. If we are to embrace the gospel of second chances, we must forgive those who may have played a role in our adversity or disappointment.

One woman in her late fifties decided that she needed to forgive her former husband who had betrayed her and abandoned their family many years earlier. She said she came to that decision when she had a sobering thought: "What if I meet him someday in the celestial kingdom?" Her children all considered that prospect laughable, but she persisted. "What if he has truly repented, and by some miracle, he is admitted into the celestial kingdom? After all, wouldn't it take something of a miracle for any of us to make it there? Then suppose I meet him in the celestial kingdom. If I haven't forgiven him, and I still have feelings of bitterness and hatred toward him, which one of us will feel the most out of place in God's presence? Wouldn't I be the one—instead of him—who's unworthy to be there?"[6]

Grudges and resentments will surely harden the heart. Bitterness is an infection of the soul. Refusing to forgive and cut others some slack, deeming them unredeemable, will slowly but surely deaden the spiritual promptings we could receive. It's been said that "harboring resentment is like taking poison and then waiting for the other person to die." When we allow ourselves to be resentful, we harm only ourselves. It has also been said that when we genuinely forgive, we set a prisoner free and then discover that we were the prisoner.

A middle-aged man learned this much too late in life. In his young adulthood, someone close to him had hurt him deeply. He carried the hurt, which festered into a grudge, for several decades. He spent years accumulating his own sort of "enemies" list, remembering others who he believed had done him wrong—most of them unknowingly or at least unintentionally. It wasn't until much later, his heart now softened by age and more of life's ups and downs, that he realized how much he had harmed himself with his own grudges. The poison of resentment had closed his heart and held him back from experiencing some of life's joys.

The solution, of course, is to let the bad feelings go. Only then is there room in our hearts for love and peace, for rewarding and lasting relationships. Emotional energy we use holding on to hurt feelings is energy we cannot use to build bonds with those we love. Rejecting the inclination to itemize hurts, slights, and offenses allows for more joy in living.

Consider the lives disrupted, the peace disturbed, the happiness destroyed by resentment. Although difficult, now is a good time to clear the heart of past hurts, to drop the "enemies" list, to step boldly into the future by letting the past go. It may not be easy, but we must give each other second chances. To relive the past is to relinquish the future. The second chances the Lord gives us depend on how we forgive or extend second chances to each other.

In a classic address, President Thomas S. Monson compared the failure to forgive to a wedge hidden in a tree, weakening its trunk and stunting its growth. He then shared an example of a humble family who made the difficult but liberating choice to forgive. Their two-month-old baby had died, and they had arranged to hold the funeral at the ward meetinghouse. On the day of the funeral, the family walked to the church, carrying the baby in a small casket. A small number of friends had gathered, but the door of the building was locked. The bishop had forgotten the funeral.

President Monson observed: "If the family were of a lesser character, they could have blamed the bishop and harbored ill feelings. When the bishop discovered the tragedy, he visited the family and apologized. With the hurt still evident in his expression, but with tears in his eyes, the father accepted the apology, and the two embraced in a spirit of understanding. No hidden wedge was left to cause further feelings of anger. Love and acceptance prevailed.

"The spirit must be freed from tethers so strong and feelings never put to rest, so that the lift of life may give buoyancy to the soul. In many families, there are hurt feelings and a reluctance to forgive. It doesn't really matter what the issue was. It cannot and should not be left to injure. Blame keeps wounds open. Only forgiveness heals. George Herbert, an early seventeenthth-century poet, wrote these lines: 'He that cannot forgive others breaks the bridge over which he himself must pass if he would ever reach heaven, for everyone has need of forgiveness.'"[7]

Breaking the bridge of forgiveness—isn't that exactly what we're doing when we refuse to forgive? In a sense, aren't we basically saying, "The Atonement may work for some people, and I expect it to work for me, but it does not work for you!" Do we dare proclaim that the Atonement is not infinite after all? And if so, how can we really be sure that it will provide forgiveness of our sins if we insist that there is no forgiveness for one who has sinned against us?

Attempting to usurp the Savior's right to judge reflects a lack of faith in the perfect justice and tender mercy of God. "Our failure to forgive will not preclude others from partaking of the fruit of the tree of life—which fruit is the love and mercy of Christ. We can only prevent ourselves from partaking of it. . . . Forgiving others opens the door for our own forgiveness of sins and our spiritual progress, and service, which could not be obtained without it."[8] Indeed, we have no power to limit the reach of the Atonement, for the Lord will forgive whom He will forgive (see D&C 64:10). Withholding our forgiveness does not really prevent anyone from receiving God's forgiveness—except ourselves.

This is the golden rule of life and relationships: extend to others the love and compassion and forgiveness you wish to have extended to you.

"FORGIVE FOR YOUR SAKE"

I continually learn this simple but profound truth, and those who live it continually inspire me. Chris Williams is one person who not only understood this principle but also lived it. In 2007 he was driving home at night with his wife and three children when their car was hit by a teenage drunk driver. Instantly, their lives changed. Chris's beloved wife, who was pregnant at the time, and two of their young children died as a result of the accident. Chris and another son survived the accident (along with a teenage son who was not in the car with them). But that's just the beginning of the story.

In the days following the accident, through his immense anguish and sorrow, a clear impression came to Chris: he must unconditionally forgive the person who had caused the tragedy. He knew it wouldn't be easy, but he knew it was the right thing to do. So he reached out to the teenage perpetrator. He did not want the young man's life to be destroyed. He did not want this accident to define the rest of his life. He wanted him to have a second chance.

Chris Williams, who was serving as a bishop at the time, knew in a very personal way that we need second chances. Years earlier, when he was a teenage driver, he had accidentally struck and killed a young boy who darted into oncoming traffic. He remembered what it was like to be a teenager all alone in the back of a police car; he remembered what it was like to go on living with the reality that he had, accidentally, ended someone's life. But his desire to forgive had even more to do with what by then had become a kind of practice. "It was almost like I had drilled myself for that moment," he said. "Forgive for your sake, not the other person's. Forgive because, if you don't, your bitterness will consume you."

Not long after the accident, Bishop Williams addressed his ward. He recounted the parable of the prodigal son and what the image of an elderly father running toward a wayward son, with arms outstretched in love, had come to mean for him. "If my Heavenly Father can treat me this way—if, when we approach Him, He runs to us—then who am I to hold a grudge, to judge another person, to not forgive?" With the empathy that often comes of experience, he had learned that forgiveness heals and empowers. Forgiveness changes everything. Through this courageous act of forgiveness, Chris Williams helped both the young man and himself move forward with life.[9]

This Is What It Means to Be a Christian

What Bishop Williams did for that teenage driver is not just a nice story about a nice man extending extraordinary kindness to someone. It is a fundamental, defining characteristic of Christian discipleship.

During the Savior's mortal ministry, He was approached by some of the leading lawyers of the day, one of whom said: "Master, which is the great commandment in the law? Jesus said unto him, Thou shalt love the Lord thy God with all thy heart, and with all thy soul, and with all thy mind. This is the first and great commandment. And the second is like unto it, Thou shalt love thy neighbour as thyself" (Matthew 22:36–39). These two commandments, He explained, are so important that all other laws and commandments rest upon them.

This was a key point that the Pharisees and lawyers had missed. They were so strict about obeying the lesser laws that they condemned the Savior's loving acts of healing because He performed them on the Sabbath. They did not understand that as important as Sabbath observance is, the commandment to keep the Sabbath day holy hangs on the two great commandments to love.

The Pharisees took pride in their knowledge of the writings of the ancient prophets, of knowing every jot and tittle of the law. But what good did that do them if they ostracized those in need of repentance and forgiveness? As important as the prophetic writings are, they also hang on the two great commandments to love. What better way to become Christlike than to do as He did—to reach out to those who have made mistakes and offer them forgiveness and love. Is there a more Christlike act? The truth is, the ability to forgive is a defining characteristic of someone who really desires to come unto Christ.

Jesus Christ gave us a new code for living—to love one another, even our enemies. He taught us to extend compassion, to refrain from judging others, to forgive, and to give others a second chance—not just once but seven times seventy, without limits (see Matthew 18:22). Christ was not teaching a mere mathematical equation, He was teaching an eternal gospel principle.

President Gordon B. Hinckley taught: "If there be any who nurture in their hearts the poisonous brew of enmity toward another, I plead with you to ask the Lord for strength to forgive. This expression of desire will be of the very substance of your repentance. It may not be easy, and it may not come quickly. But if you will seek it with sincerity and cultivate it, it *will* come. . . . There will come into your heart a peace otherwise unattainable."[10]

People like Chris Williams bring such Christian principles to life. You and I are called to do the same. We are called to transcend ourselves in love, kindness, care, and compassion and, in doing so, grow in likeness to God.

THE PRODIGAL BROTHER

Who among us has not been in need of forgiveness? Who has not been lost? Whether as a child with tear-stained cheeks, a teenager who thought he knew the way, or a weary traveler, fumbling to make sense of a map—we've all been lost. Hopefully, we've all been found. The joy of being found, or of finding oneself, is unsurpassed—especially when, like the prodigal, we've been lost to our true and best self. It wasn't until the prodigal son "came to himself" (Luke 15:17) and began to catch sight of who he really was that he found his way back home. With a humble and penitent heart, he discovered true happiness.

We often emphasize the return of the prodigal in this parable—understandably so, because it is a poignant moment that gives hope to all of us who have had our prodigal times. We need always to remember that the father—our Father—stands at the door, looking as far down the road as he can, anxious to see any sign that we want to come home again, and as soon as he does, he will come running.

But as powerful as that message is, I don't think it was Jesus's primary point in telling this parable. His immediate audience, you'll remember, was a group of Pharisees and scribes who were indignant over the fact that sinners were attracted to Jesus and that He received them (see Luke 15:1–2). It was in response to this murmuring that Jesus told the parable of the prodigal son.

These Pharisees and scribes probably felt that they identified best with the older brother in this parable—the dutiful one who stayed home and never indulged in riotous living as his brother had. But what this son (and the Pharisees and scribes) failed to understand was that he was just as much a prodigal as his brother was. He had lost his way—not in a far country like his wayward brother but at home, in the fog of selfishness, jealousy, and anger. When the older brother returned from the fields and heard the music and dancing at his brother's welcome-home party, the older brother asked one of the servants what was happening. The servant explained that his wayward brother had returned, and their father had ordered a celebration. But the older brother "was angry, and would not go in" (Luke 15:28). He stayed outside and pouted until his father entreated him. True, the younger son had wandered far from his father, but he came back. The older son showed—through his anger and unwillingness to rejoice over his brother's return—that he had, in a sense, wandered far from his loving father as well. Although he did not recognize it, the older brother was also in need of a second chance.

In a sense, we're all prodigals, lost from our Heavenly Father, unless we walk the path of repentance and forgiveness. The prophet Isaiah wrote, "All we like sheep have gone astray" (Isaiah 53:6). Spiritually more than geographically, we sometimes go astray and detour from the gospel path. But if we're to be found, we must first realize that we're lost.

In a subtle act of mercy, Jesus leaves open the ending of this parable. It closes with the father pleading with the older son to change his heart and rejoice at his brother's return: "It was meet that we should make merry, and be glad: for this thy brother was dead, and is alive again; and was lost, and is found" (Luke 15:32). We do not hear how the older brother responds to his father's entreaty, because that's a question the scribes and Pharisees needed to answer for themselves—and one that we must answer for ourselves as well. How will we respond when the prodigal returns? Will we see him only in terms of his sins and his past and resent any forgiveness he receives? Or will we "make merry, and be glad"?

We Need Each Other

Have you ever thought about how much easier it is to be kind and patient, charitable and compassionate when you're alone? At least, it seems easier. In reality, it's impossible. You could move alone to a mountaintop and study scriptures and fast and pray all day, but you would never develop the depth of spirituality and love that comes only in our sometimes difficult interactions with each other. It's not only going to church and attending the temple that teach us how to love; it is keeping the covenants and living the principles of the gospel in our daily life. Spirituality comes not of being a hermit but of living with and interacting with others, who can be exasperating, frustrating, and annoying at times. It is in relation to others that we learn patience, long-suffering, and compassion.

Isn't that why we have families? Heavenly Father didn't send us here alone; He sent us into family groups that not only mirror the organization of heaven but also require us to figure out how to get along with each other (see Genesis 2:18). In families we bump into each other, we sometimes annoy one another, and we may even offend one another. But it is also in families that we learn—in a way that would be impossible otherwise—how to love, how to forgive, and how to sacrifice.

I believe this is one reason the Lord's Church is organized into wards. In many churches, worshippers attend any congregation they want, often basing their choice on the location of the chapel, the schedule of the worship service, or the speaking style of the minister. The Lord has not given Latter-day Saints that luxury. We attend church at the meetinghouse assigned to our ward (even if another meetinghouse might be closer). And if our ward is assigned the 9:00–12:00 meeting block, that's the one we attend, no matter how hard it might be to get up that early on a Sunday. And, as any Latter-day Saint will attest, speakers in sacrament meeting are not chosen for their public speaking skills. But what other churches gain in personal convenience comes at the potential cost of a sense of community among worshippers. Members of a Latter-day Saint ward can become almost like a family—with family-like love and concern, along with occasional family-like problems and disagreements.

This seems to be the way the Lord wants it. He wants us to feel responsibility for each other. He wants us to notice when someone is missing. He wants us to learn not to offend one another and not to take offense. But if offenses come, He wants us to learn to forgive and allow each other a second chance.

He knows that on this mortal journey, we need each other.

Elder Joseph B. Wirthlin said: "The Church is not a place where perfect people gather to say perfect things, or have perfect thoughts, or have perfect feelings. The Church is a place where imperfect people gather to provide encouragement, support, and service to each other as we press on in our journey to return to our Heavenly Father."[11]

It is in our service to others that we manifest our commitment to Christ. "Today the most visible strength of The Church of Jesus Christ of Latter-day Saints is the unselfish service and sacrifice of its members," said Elder Dallin H. Oaks. "Prior to the dedication of one of our temples, a Christian minister asked President Gordon B. Hinckley why it did not contain any representation of the cross, the most common symbol of the Christian faith. President Hinckley replied that the symbols of *our* Christian faith are 'the lives of our people.' Truly, our lives of service and sacrifice are the most appropriate expressions of our commitment to serve the Master and our fellowmen."[12]

We're all in this together. In fellowship with the household of faith, we join together to mourn with those who mourn, comfort those who need comfort, and stand as witnesses of God at all times and in all places (see Mosiah 18:9). We rejoice in positive growth and righteous change whenever and wherever we see it.

We don't always see eye to eye, and in some cases our differences seem to outweigh our similarities, but we have one thing in common that transcends everything else: We all need the Atonement of Christ. Here's how the Apostle Paul explained it during a time when the Church was beginning to gather in people from a diversity of nationalities, backgrounds, and cultures:

"At that time [before receiving the gospel] ye were without Christ, being aliens from the commonwealth of Israel, and strangers from the covenants of promise, having no hope, and without God in the world:

"But now in Christ Jesus ye who sometimes were far off are made nigh by the blood of Christ.

"For he is our peace, who hath made both one, and hath broken down the middle wall of partition between us;

"Having abolished in his flesh the enmity, . . . to make in himself of twain one new man, so making peace" (Ephesians 2:12–15).

May we allow the Atonement of Jesus Christ to unite and humble us, to break down the walls that separate us, abolishing pride and enmity, that where we have been far apart, we can be one, "so making peace."

ALWAYS THERE IS HOPE

The power of the Atonement and the principle of repentance
show that we should never give up on loved ones who
now seem to be making many wrong choices.

DALLIN H. OAKS

Not long ago, a friend stopped by to see me. It didn't take long to sense he had come for more than small talk. His slumped shoulders, tired eyes, and wearied tone spoke nonverbal volumes. After a few minutes of casual conversation, he told me about his daughter who was making some bad decisions and seemed to be leaving the gospel path. Worried and heartbroken, my friend expressed the tender feelings of his heart: "I wonder what we could have done differently, what we did wrong. I think about where she's headed, and the pain she's causing—and the pain ahead of her—and I can't sleep at night. I worry that she'll become so lost that she'll never find her way back to us, to the gospel, to happiness." He told me how hard it was to go to church on Sunday and hear testimonies and talks about children on missions, children getting married in the temple, children who seem so faithful and so strong and so on course. His emotions ranged from sorrow to anger to helplessness. Unspoken, but all too clear, was the poignant question "Is there hope for her?"

What do you say to help a person in a situation like this? It's easy to fall back on pat answers and quick fixes, simple homilies that may be true but are often not all that helpful. In this case, what I tried to do was listen. Not lecture or pontificate or recommend. Just listen.

He knew what he needed to do.

This was a good brother who loved the Lord, who with his wife sincerely tried to rear his children in light and truth, who did his best to live the gospel with fervent conviction. But things didn't turn out as he and his wife had planned. We talked about the plan of happiness and mercy, about agency and choice, about faith and hope, about the Atonement and redemption, about the gospel of second chances. I bore my testimony to him of the love of God, of the infinite and eternal atoning sacrifice of the Savior, and of my love and respect for him, and I expressed my willingness to walk beside him.

Good has come even of his heartache. He said to me, "My prayers have never been as sincere as they are now. I've never pleaded with the Lord so strongly. My temple attendance is more regular. Now I come to sacrament meeting with a broken heart and a contrite spirit. My heart has been humbled; my empathy for others has increased. I'm a better person than I was—more patient, understanding, compassionate, and forgiving. I've come to *really* understand what I've always known: things and possessions don't matter at all. My hope and faith are in Christ and His

Atonement. I love my family, and my daughter with all my heart. More than anything else, I want us to be together forever."

Of this I know and testify: The final chapter in his daughter's life and in his, has not been written. For them, and for each of us, always there is hope.

Always—a second chance.

Notes

Chapter 1: A Message of Hope

1. "The Ancient Sage," in *Poems of Tennyson,* ed. Henry Van Dyke and D. Laurance Chambers (Boston, Mass.: Ginn & Company, 1903), 263.

2. Harold Kushner, *Conquering Fear: Living Boldly in an Uncertain World* (New York: Anchor Books, 2009), 93–94.

3. Monson, "Be of Good Cheer," *Ensign,* May 2009, 92.

4. "When Faith Endures," *Hymns of The Church of Jesus Christ of Latter-day Saints* (Salt Lake City: The Church of Jesus Christ of Latter-day Saints, 1985), no. 128.

Chapter 2: The Gospel's Central Message

Hafen, "Eve Heard All These Things and Was Glad," in *Women in the Covenant of Grace,* ed. Dawn Hall Fletcher and Susette Fletcher Green (Salt Lake City: Deseret Book, 1994), 32.

1. President David O. McKay said, "The purpose of the gospel is . . .

to make bad men good and good men better, and to change human nature." Conference Report, Apr. 1954, 26.

2. Uchtdorf, "A Matter of a Few Degrees," *Ensign,* May 2008, 60.

3. Emily Watts, "Life Is Too Short: You Have Reached Your Destination," *LDS Living,* January/February 2012, 95.

Chapter 3: God Wants Us to Believe in Second Chances

1. Interestingly, the curse given to Laman's posterity almost appears to have built into it the promise of a second chance. Consider these words of blessing from Lehi to Laman's children: "If ye are cursed, behold, I leave my blessing upon you, that the cursing may be taken from you and be answered upon the heads of your parents. Wherefore, because of my blessing the Lord God will not suffer that ye shall perish; wherefore, he will be merciful unto you and unto your seed forever" (2 Nephi 4:6–7). The sons of Mosiah were clearly instruments in the Lord's hands in fulfilling this promise of mercy toward Lehi's seed. The Lord continues to fulfill this promise today as modern missionaries take the gospel to the children of Lehi.

2. Uceda, "Jonah and the Second Chance," *Ensign,* Sept. 2002, 26.

3. Quoted in Richard E. Turley and William W. Slaughter, *How We Got the Book of Mormon* (Salt Lake City: Deseret Book, 2011), 19.

4. Packer, "The Least of These," *Ensign,* Nov. 2004, 87; emphasis added.

5. Packer, "Least of These," 87.

Chapter 4: Second Chances Are for Everyone

Teachings of the Prophet Joseph Smith, sel. Joseph Fielding Smith (Salt Lake City: Deseret Book, 1976), 191.

1. C. S. Lewis argued against what he called the "silly idea" that "good people do not know what temptation means. This is an obvious

lie," he said. "Only those who try to resist temptation know how strong it is. After all, you find out the strength of the German army by fighting against it, not by giving in. You find out the strength of a wind by trying to walk against it, not by lying down. A man who gives in to temptation after five minutes simply does not know what it would have been like an hour later. That is why bad people, in one sense, know very little about badness. They have lived a sheltered life by always giving in. We never find out the strength of the evil impulse inside us until we try to fight it: and Christ, because He was the only man who never yielded to temptation, is also the only man who knows to the full what temptation means" (*Mere Christianity* [New York: Macmillan, 1960], 109–10).

2. Bednar, "The Atonement and the Journey of Mortality," *Ensign,* Apr. 2012, 47.

3. Grace is a "divine means of help or strength, given through the bounteous mercy and love of Jesus Christ. It is through the grace of the Lord Jesus, made possible by his atoning sacrifice, that mankind will be raised in immortality, every person receiving his body from the grave in a condition of everlasting life. It is likewise through the grace of the Lord that individuals, through faith in the atonement of Jesus Christ and repentance of their sins, receive strength and assistance to do good works that they otherwise would not be able to maintain if left to their own means. This grace is an enabling power that allows men and women to lay hold on eternal life and exaltation after they have expended their own best efforts. Divine grace is needed by every soul in consequence of the fall of Adam and also because of man's weaknesses and shortcomings. However, grace cannot suffice without total effort on the part of the recipient. Hence the explanation, 'It is by grace that we are saved, after all we can do' (2 Ne. 25:23). It is truly the grace of Jesus Christ that makes salvation possible" (LDS Bible Dictionary, s.v. "Grace," 697).

Chapter 5: Acknowledging the Need to Change

1. In William E. Phipps, *Amazing Grace in John Newton: Slave-Ship Captain, Hymnwriter, and Abolitionist* (Macon, Ga.: Mercer University Press, 2001), 4. The 2006 movie *Amazing Grace* provides an exceptional portrayal of the life of William Wilberforce and his interaction with John Newton.

2. Quoted in Phipps, *Amazing Grace,* 209.

3. Bernard Martin, *John Newton: A Biography* (London: Heinemann, 1950), 364.

4. John Newton, "Hymn XLI," *Amazing Grace: An Anthology of Poems about Slavery,* ed. James G. Basker (New Haven, Conn.: Yale University Press, 2005), 281–82.

5. A hypocrite is someone who acts or pretends to be righteous but really is not. The word comes from the Greek *hypokrites,* which means "actor." Misuse of the term *hypocrite* is, unfortunately, widespread. Too many genuinely good people are accused of being hypocrites because they are imperfect. And this leads to an even worse problem: too many resist making positive changes in their spiritual lives because they know they cannot be perfect and they fear that others will see them as hypocrites. We must be clear on this: a hypocrite is one who performs righteous acts in public for the purpose of putting on a show—to gain favor or praise from others—and has no corresponding desire for righteousness in the heart (see Matthew 6:1–6; 23:25–28). A person who is genuinely trying to do and be good but falls short is not a hypocrite.

6. See also Romans 3:10; 1 John 1:8–10; Ecclesiastes 7:20.

7. Robert L. Millet, "Joseph Smith Encounters Calvinism," *BYU Studies* 50, no. 4 (2011): 10.

8. Hafen, "The Atonement: All for All," *Ensign,* May 2004, 97.

9. Callister, *The Infinite Atonement* (Salt Lake City: Deseret Book, 2000), 177–78.

10. D. Todd Christofferson, "The Divine Gift of Repentance," *Ensign,* Nov. 2011, 38.

11. Interestingly, even though Nehor was executed, the influence of his philosophy endured—cropping up, for example, among the people of Ammonihah, who were "of the profession of Nehor" (Alma 16:11). It was a resident of Ammonihah, the lawyer Zeezrom, who before he was converted argued with Amulek about whether God would save His people *in* their sins or *from* their sins (see Alma 11:34–37).

12. Young, in *Journal of Discourses,* 26 vols. (London: Latter-day Saints' Book Depot, 1854–86), 8:124–25.

13. Monson, "May We So Live," *Ensign,* Aug. 2008, 7.

14. Packer, "The Brilliant Morning of Forgiveness," *Ensign,* Nov. 1995, 20.

15. Whitney, in Conference Report, April 1929, 110; emphasis added.

Chapter 6: Acknowledging the Possibility of Change

Teachings of the Prophet Joseph Smith, sel. Joseph Fielding Smith (Salt Lake City: Deseret Book, 1976), 257.

1. *Bartlett's Familiar Quotations,* ed. Justin Kaplan, 16th ed. (Boston: Little, Brown, and Company, 1992), 694.

2. Packer, "The Brilliant Morning of Forgiveness," *Ensign,* Nov. 1995, 20.

3. Monson, "Anxiously Engaged," *Ensign,* Nov. 2004, 58.

4. Faust, "The Power to Change," *Ensign,* Nov. 2007, 122–24.

5. Holland, "The Laborers in the Vineyard," *Ensign,* May 2012, 32–33.

6. Edison, in *Quote This! A Collection of Illustrated Quotes for Educators,* ed. Diane Hodges (Thousand Oaks, Calif.: Corwin Press, 2008), 70.

7. Maxwell, "Notwithstanding My Weakness," *Ensign,* Nov. 1976, 14.

8. *Teachings of Gordon B. Hinckley* (Salt Lake City: Deseret Book, 1997), 160.

9. Lewis, *Mere Christianity* (New York: Macmillan, 1960), 172–73. Lewis explains that people get this way through "good infection" from personal contact with Christ (*Mere Christianity,* 138).

10. Packer, *Let Not Your Heart Be Troubled* (Salt Lake City: Bookcraft, 1991), 292.

11. Oaks, "Powerful Ideas," *Ensign,* Nov. 1995, 25.

12. Monson, "Yellow Canaries with Gray on Their Wings," *Ensign,* Aug. 1987, 2.

13. *The Neal A. Maxwell Quote Book,* ed. Cory H. Maxwell (Salt Lake City: Bookcraft, 1997), 243.

14. Uchtdorf, "Your Happily Ever After," *Ensign,* May 2010, 125.

15. Uchtdorf, "Your Happily Ever After," 126.

16. Adapted from *Music and the Spoken Word,* "An Unfinished Book," message 4023.

17. *Bartlett's Familiar Quotations,* ed. Justin Kaplan, 17th ed. (Boston: Little, Brown, and Company, 2002), 319.

18. Ralph Waldo Emerson, in James Elliot Cabot, *A Memoir of Ralph Waldo Emerson,* 6th ed., 2 vols. (Boston: Houghton Mifflin, 1887), 2:489.

19. Lewis, *The Last Battle* (New York: HarperTrophy, 1956), 210–11.

20. "Why Faith Matters," *Parade,* Sept. 12, 2010, 22.

21. *Church News,* May 8, 2010, 15.

22. Among other excellent examples in literature of second chances, to name but a few, are Victor Hugo's *Les Misérables,* Jane Austen's *Persuasion* and *Pride and Prejudice,* several of Shakespeare's plays, and nearly all of Charles Dickens's books.

Chapter 7: Acknowledging Our Dependence on the Savior

1. See Matthew 19:16–26; Mark 10:17–27; Luke 18:18–27.
2. Millet, "Joseph Smith Encounters Calvinism," *BYU Studies* 50, no. 4 (2011): 28.

Chapter 8: Making the Second Chance Last

In Tryon Edwards, ed., *A Dictionary of Thoughts* (Detroit, Mich: F. B. Dickerson, 1908), 149.

1. Holland, "The Best Is Yet to Be," *Ensign,* Jan. 2010, 24.
2. Bowen, "The Atonement Can Clean, Reclaim, and Sanctify Our Lives," *Ensign,* Nov. 2006, 33.
3. J. Spencer Kinard, *A Time for Reflection* (Salt Lake City: Deseret Book, 1986), 4–5.
4. Evans, in Conference Report, Oct. 1969, 68.
5. Faust, "Stand Up and Be Counted," *Ensign,* Feb. 1982, 71.
6. Beck, quoting Lynn G. Robbins, in "For the Strength of You," *Ensign,* Oct. 2007, 17.
7. Benson, "A Mighty Change of Heart," *Ensign,* Oct. 1989, 2.
8. Erik Kolbell, *The God of Second Chances* (Louisville, Ky.: Westminster John Knox Press, 2008), 23.
9. Oaks, "The Challenge to Become," *Ensign,* Nov. 2000, 32.
10. Cannon, in *Millennial Star* 25 (Oct. 4, 1863): 722.
11. See Matthew 10:22; 24:13; Mark 13:13; 2 Timothy 2:10; James 5:11; 1 Nephi 13:37; 3 Nephi 15:9; 27:16–17; Doctrine and Covenants 6:13; 14:7; 18:22; 20:25, 29; 50:5; 101:35.

Chapter 9: Giving Others a Second Chance

Dieter F. Uchtdorf, "The Merciful Obtain Mercy," *Ensign,* May 2012, 75.

1. *Merriam-Webster's Collegiate Dictionary,* 11th ed. (Springfield, Mass.: Merriam-Webster, 2001), s.v. "scrooge."

2. *Collegiate Dictionary,* s.v. "grinch."

3. Holland, "The Best Is Yet to Be," *Ensign,* Jan. 2010, 26.

4. Osguthorpe, "When Love Is Why," *BYU Magazine,* Fall 2011; available online at http://magazine.byu.edu/?act=view&a=2886.

5. *John Taylor,* Teachings of Presidents of the Church series (Salt Lake City: The Church of Jesus Christ of Latter-day Saints, 2001), 21.

6. Of course, someone who has truly repented would make those he betrayed part of his journey to repentance. If he has not tried to make amends in his own family, he's not going to be able to sneak into the celestial kingdom. But to this faithful woman, that was beside the point. She did not consider it her place to decide whether or not *he* had fully repented; rather, she was concerned about whether *she* had fully repented of her own feelings of bitterness toward her former husband.

7. Monson, "Hidden Wedges," *Ensign,* May 2002, 19.

8. Robert L. Millet, Camille Fronk Olson, Andrew C. Skinner, Brent L. Top, *LDS Beliefs: A Doctrinal Reference* (Salt Lake City: Deseret Book, 2011), 238.

9. See Chris Williams, *Let It Go: A True Story of Tragedy and Forgiveness* (Salt Lake City: Deseret Book, 2012).

10. *Teachings of Gordon B. Hinckley* (Salt Lake City: Deseret Book, 1997), 229.

11. Wirthlin, "The Virtue of Kindness," *Ensign,* May 2005, 28.

12. Oaks, "Sacrifice," *Ensign,* May 2012, 19–20.

EPILOGUE: ALWAYS THERE IS HOPE

Oaks, "The Challenge to Become," *Ensign,* Nov. 2000, 34.

INDEX